HELMETS, HANDCUFFS HOSES

The Story of The Wallasey Police and Fire Brigade
Part Two

WALLASEY FIRE BRIGADE

by
Noel E Smith

Published by the Author:
"Sandheys" 164 Rake Lane,
Wallasey CH45 1JP
Tel: 0151 639 6923

Design and Origination:
Ian Boumphrey
Tel/Fax: 0151 608 7611
e-mail: ian@yesterdayswirral.co.uk

Printed by:
Printfine Ltd Gibraltar Row Liverpool L3 7HJ
Tel: 0151 242 0000 Website: www.printfine.co.uk

**Price
£6.95**

ISBN: 0-9517762-4-X

Early History of Firefighting

Firefighters have existed for many years. In about 510 to 82 BC bands of slaves were used to fight fires. They were called Familia Publica who were stationed by the City Gates and along the walls. The first Firefighters would have used leather buckets and it was not until Emperor Augustus took measures after many buildings were destroyed by fire in Rome in AD 6 that he set about organising the first highly trained Fire Brigade, the *Corps of Vigiles*. They were each responsible for an area of Rome, there being 14 areas in all. There were 1,000 men in each area under the command of a centurion. The men had to be prepared to serve for 26 years but they could leave after six. Small houses were built for them. Their duty was to patrol the streets of a night acting as a sort of policeman during the hours of darkness and they were equipped with an axe and bucket. These were the forerunners of the Police-Firemen in this country many years later. The Vigiles would use water bags which were made of animal skins and could be thrown into the fire. They also cut down branches from the nearby trees and used them as beaters. With their long hooks, they were able to pull away burning material from the roofs and walls. They had Dolebrae or pick axes to break down doors and the like; blankets were dipped into water and thrown over the flames; ladders or scalae were used to rescue people from upper windows. They used a simple type of pump and were later equipped with large brass syringes known as 'Squirts' which two men held while the third operated the plunger.

The Corps were divided into 'cohorts' or companies which were commanded by a 'Syphonarius' who was in charge of the pumping appliance. Other titles were 'aquarius' – this was a water carrier who kept the pump or 'siphos' and 'uncinarius' – a hook man.

Ring forth ye bells
With clarion sound

WS Gilbert

Long fire-hooks were used to to pull down the
burning thatch to stop the fire spreading

In this country a bell would be rung when there was afire. The Fire Bell was used at Canterbury in AD 24. Church bells were also used to muster villagers to the fire which would ring the bells in reverse peal.

Firefighting commenced in Britain during the reign of King Alfred and in Norman times there was a nightly curfew bell which when rung the inhabitants had to cover their fires. This was known as *Couvre Feu* from which we get the word 'curfew'. This law was not popular with householders and was repealed in the time of Henry I (AD1100 - 1135). They were, however, still obliged to keep a bucket of water by the fire. The Great Fire of London was

Sketch of the Great Fire of London

responsible for the loss of 3,000 lives in 1212, many being trapped on London Bridge as the fire spread from both ends. Steps were taken to prevent fires and controls were introduced.

The first wheeled Fire Engine was developed by Alan Plater as early as 1518. Buckets and squirts were the norm of the day for most parts of the country followed by the simple hand-operated pump.

A Fire Engine of sorts was paraded in the City of London's Lord Mayor's Show in 1548.

In 1625, Roger Jones patented a Fire Appliance and a two-man Manual Engine was produced in the following year. It did not have wheels so had to be carried like a stretcher with the aid of poles and shoulder straps. In 1652 the City of Exeter obtained a fire vehicle.

The second Great Fire of London happened in September 1666 with colossal results. Well over 13,000 houses were burnt to the ground as well as 89 churches and 52 halls. St Paul's Cathedral, the Guildhall and other prominent buildings went up in flames. Countless thousands of folk were left homeless but casualties were few. The fire lasted for four days. It all started in a baker's shop in Pudding Lane while the baker, Mr Frayor, was asleep in bed he was awakened by a man knocking and shouting. The baker and his family managed to climb on to the roof and escape but their maid servant, who was too afraid to follow, perished being one of the first persons to die as a result of the fire.

The good thing that came out of the fire was the fact it cleared away the diseases of the Great Plague that had ravaged London in 1665.

In most English villages fires had to be put out by use of the humble bucket. A line of people would pass them along from the source of water – a horse-trough, pond or brook.

Acts of 1707 and 1774 required every parish to provide horse-drawn engines, hoses and ladders. With all probability, the first Fire Engines were those of 1707 (Hand-in-Hand), 1716 (Sun Fire Office) and 1720 (Westminster Fire Office).

A Volunteer Fire Brigade was established at Chester in 1709 and a Fire Engine House was built for five hand-operated pumps. A new one was built in 1761 and soon there were thirty Firemen.

Some old churches have interesting relics. For instance, at Worlingworth in Suffolk there is an ancient Fire Engine of 1760 and at Kislingbury, Northamptonshire, there are eight fire buckets bearing the date 1743. Other churches have long fire-hooks that could be borrowed for pulling down the burning thatch from the cottages in the village.

Rewards were offered to the first Fire Engine to arrive at a fire. Scottish cities took measures in setting up fire regulations in the early 1800s establishing proper fire brigades.

Normally brigades did not charge for attending a fire but Manchester Council allowed their brigade to make a charge of £15. In 1824, the insurance company fire brigades in Edinburgh came under central control forming the Edinburgh Fire Engine Establishment with James Braidwood in command. The men wore blue jackets and canvas trousers, leather helmets styled on the pattern of the New Zealanders and an additional leather flap hung over the back of the helmet to prevent falling matter injuring the Fireman.

London Fire Brigade dates from 1833. Prior to that date, brigades were maintained by insurance companies to protect properties that were insured by them against fire. One of the first companies was that of the Hope Insurance Company whose Firemen dressed in red and blue with helmets made of leather for head protection. James Braidwood left his post in Scotland to become Superintendent of the newly formed London Brigade. Other brigades followed within five years. The blue clad men of the Sun Insurance Company were well-known by their large badge of a face of a shining sun with the word 'Sun Fire Officer' above. This company is now the Sun Alliance Insurance Group. They had Liverpool offices in Bank Buildings and Craig's Court in 1807. Mr C Pole was agent for the office at 7 Old Church Yard.

The insurance companies would fix a badge and number of the policy on the wall of insured buildings. These were originally made of lead but were changed to copper or iron. Examples of these can be seen in Chester. Their brigades were equipped with handcarts, ladders, leather buckets and squirts.

Merryweather produced hose and ladder carts which were hauled manually and used by the insurance companies. They carried a short extension ladder, a couple of squirts and about a dozen leather buckets. A later model carried a hydrant stand-pipe and a reel of canvas hose.

The oldest of these insurance Brigades was the Amicable Contributionship (Hand-in-Hand) which was founded in 1696. The Phoenix, Sun Fire Office and Royal Exchange Assurance Company combined to fight fires in 1791 and were joined in 1826 by the London Assurance. The Firemen were part-timers but soon became full-time.

An 18th Century act ordered the churchwardens to maintain at least one engine in every parish, and ladders to aid escape. They were also ordered to fix stop blocks and fire plugs at convenient distances upon all the main pipes in the parish, to place a mark in the street where they could be found, and to have a key ready to open the plugs, so that water might be easily obtained in case of fire.

In 1829 John Braithwaite and John Ericsson built the first Steam Fire pump which was able to pump 150 gallons a minute and had a great advantage in winter as they did not freeze up. This invention did away with having men on hand-pumps who would often cut the hoses because they feared that they would lose their beer

An early fire engine

ration. Not all small towns and villages had Fire Engines but relied on the humble hose-cart where the hose was wound around a pair of wheels or the axle. Stand pipes, branches, buckets and perhaps a ladder made up the equipment.

Smoke was always a problem when fighting fires as the men could be suffocated and as early as the eighteenth century smoke masks were invented. These were a hood that had a snout attached to a length of pipe for fresh air.

The French produced a coat with hood attached and a window to enable the Firemen to see what he was doing. A belt around the waist made the top of the coat airtight with a pipe attached to this portion which ran to a bellows unit that was activated for the flow of fresh air. This was known as the 'Pauline Apparel'. Another mask that was used in the 1800s was the 'Roberts' hood and mouthpiece. The leather hood was made airtight around the neck by means of padded cotton and from the helmet hung a sort of pipe of some 30 inches in length with a trumpet-shaped bell at the end which held a filter formed from a sponge that was soaked in water. The pipe had a couple of tabs attached with button holes which enabled the equipment to be fastened to the buttons of the tunic.

In about 1840, Firemen started to wear shorter coats when the badge was worn on the chest instead of the arm and volunteer firemen would either pay for their own uniform or it was provided by public subscription.

The Liverpool Salvage Corps was established in 1842 being funded by the insurance companies with their headquarters in Hatton Garden. Their job was to recover goods and to minimise loss at commercial buildings as result of fire or other peril.

In 1843 the Liverpool Warehouse Act was passed which aimed at making buildings less vulnerable to outbreaks of fire. Certain restrictions were made regarding window openings and wooden structures that had been erected too near the main buildings. To encourage owners of warehouses, the insurance companies offered lower premiums if they built their warehouses of inflammable materials. Flour mills and corn warehouses were then built of brick with small windows but they were still subject to fires.

Hand syringe 1666

In about 1850, Brigades started to replace their leather hoses with the canvas type.

In 1858 Shand, Mason and Company introduced a heavily-built three Horse-Drawn Steam Engine and the prime Fire Engine manufacturing firm of Merryweather and Sons of London brought out their first Steam Fire Engine. They were, with Shand, Mason and another firm called Roberts and Baddeley, soon producing manual Engines which were also exported. Merryweather and Sons produced a Steam Engine in 1861 which they named 'Deluge'. The Horse-drawn Merryweather Manual Pumps were called 'Paxtons'. Over the next few years other Fire Engines appeared on the market.

James braidwood invented a fire escape for which he was awarded a silver medal by the London Society of Arts and the same body invited him to write an account of his mode of drilling firemen and dealing with fires. He was not only a skillful organiser, but he also possessed great presence of mind and an unusual amount of personal courage. During a severe fire at a warehouse in 1861 a terrible explosion took place resulting in the whole of the front of the warehouse collapsing causing the death of Braidwood and another fireman. Throughout the day of the funeral, the bells of the city churches boomed slowly. The queen sent a message of sympathy to his widow.

Police Brigades were set up in various parts of the country with the idea of saving money. The Chester Police had taken over the Fire Brigade in the city in 1803 and in 1846 they built a Fire Station in Northgate Street but by 1853 the Police resigned as Firemen as they found the work too onerous. They 'walked out' as they were expected to wash the engines during their off-duty hours. Eventually, the situation was sorted out. In 1863 the City of Chester Volunteer Fire Brigade was formed with seven Officers and 60 Firemen. The Brigade would not tolerate the men using bad language on duty and those heard doing so were fined five shillings. By 1870, the Chester Brigade had a Horse-Drawn Manual Engine and a Wheeled Ladder and in addition, a Hand-Drawn Manual Engine. These were kept in a new Fire Engine House in Northgate Street. In 1895 the brigade bought a Merryweather Steamer.

50ft.Wheeled-Escapes were becoming common with Brigades around the country.

On the fire that glows
with heat intense
I turn the hose
of common sense
And out it goes
At small expense!
We must maintain our fairy law;
That is the main
on which to draw –
In that we gain
A captain Shaw!
Oh, Captain Shaw!
Type of true love kept under!
Could thy Brigade
With cold cascade
Quench my great love, I wonder!

The above verses from Gilbert & Sullivan's Iolanthe (produced in 1882) were given to the fairy queen to sing the praises of Captain Shaw, the Superintendent of the London Fire brigade and which delighted the London public. Even present day firemen receive advice from Captain Shaw, for the *Manual of Firemanship,* issued under the authority of the Home Office offers practical firemanship. Sir Massey Shaw wrote in his book

Fires and Fire Brigades: "A fireman to be successful must enter buildings; he must get in below, above, on every side, from opposite houses, over back walls, through panels of doors, through windows, through loop holes, through skylights, through holes cut by himself in gates, the walls, the roof; he must know how to reach the attic from the basement by ladders placed on half-burnt stairs, and the basement from the attic by a rope made fast to a chimney. His whole success depends in his getting in and remaining there and he must always carry his appliance with him, as without it he is of no use".

The words, though penned many years ago are as true now as the day they were written.

In 1866, by Act of Parliament 1865, the London Fire Engine Establishment eventually became the Metropolitan Fire Brigade (paid by the Government, County and insurance companies) in 1904 under the leadership of Captain Eyre-Massey Shaw who introduced the famous French brass helmet of the Sapeurs-Pompiers. The purpose of them being made of polished brass was so that they would shine in a fire. The same principal that the illuminative strips on the Firemen's tunics do today.

The pattern used by English Fire Brigades had a peak back and front. The helmet had a leather interior and brass chin chain sewn on leather. The Firemen of the Metropolitan Fire Brigade in Victorian times had been sailors as these were thought to be the best candidates for the Fire Service. They had a good devotion to duty and had been used to discipline. When they joined the Fire Brigade, they still used the seagoing terms such as 'watches', 'mess' and 'crews'. These terms are still used by the Fire Brigades in this country. The Firemen had a traditional call of "Hi-Ya-Hi" as they raced to a fire. This is said to be a call used by sailors of old. The Firemen started to wear blue uniform in place of the grey and a sailor's hat. Permission was given in 1867 for parishes to form Fire Brigades. Volunteer Steam Brigades were set up in the 1870s and the Fire Brigades Association came into being.

Merryweather had brought out a Horse-Drawn Manual Pump in the 1870s that a 6-inch Merryweather engine which was operated by, if possible, 30 men which was capable of producing 100 gpm at one stroke per second.

In 1880, Shand Mason introduced a new patented escape and brought out a Horse-Drawn Steam Pump in 1893. The inch and three quarter jet could rise as high as 160 feet at a rate of 350 gpm. It was a common sight to see a Fire Engine racing along the streets with smoke belching out of the funnel and the crew holding on to the rail. The turntable ladder was developed in 1892 by the German company of Magris that could rise to 90ft. It was mounted on a horse-drawn vehicle. The Chemical Engines came in around about the turn of the century.

The First Steam Fire Engine

The burnt out shell of St Hilary's Church, Wallasey, is pictured after the fire in February 1857. When the Church was rebuilt in 1859 the surviving tower remained separate from the new building

In 1904 the first Motor Fire Engine was introduced. Manufactured by Merryweather with a Hatfield 500-gpm pump which was driven by the vehicle's engine. A 60 gallon water tank was on board and it carried a 50ft. Wheeled Escape.

Dennis Brothers of Guildford had been bicycle manufacturers before entering the motor industry. They built their first fire engine in 1908 using a Gwynnes Pump. The centrifugal pump had a rotating vane instead of the usual pistons to develop the pressure. This appliance was purchased by the Bradford Fire Brigade. The sale encouraged Dennis Brothers to build fire engines using the powerful turbine Tamini pump which was capable of delivering 500 gallons of water per minute. The Aster engine was replaced with the White and Poppe engine.

Early brigades would use a bugle or a post horn to warn the public and it was not until 1905 that a gong or bell was operated by an Officer on the Engine which became universal.

The dark blue waterproof uniform became popular in the 1880s and the boots were of the Napoleon and Wellington style. Trousers were tucked into the tops of their boots. Brigades adopted the brass helmet of the London Fire Brigade in the place of, or addition to, the sailor-type hat (Wallasey did likewise). In some instances, the hat ribbon carried the name of the Fire Brigade in the same way the sailor had the name of his ship. The buttons of their coats were ornamented with two crossed hatchets. Some Firemen wore a light cap under the helmet and carried a hank of rope. Each man had a number which was displayed on the left side of the chest. On the shoulders of the tunic there were epaulettes or strips of metal to protect the wearers when hit by falling objects. The Firemen then were on duty 24 hours a day for 14 days and nights, except when off sick. Every 15th day was free but they still could be called upon if there was a serious fire and more men were needed.

******

Firefighting in Wallasey

It's quite honorary
The trade that we ply

WS Gilbert

No one knows when the first firefighting force was set up in Wallasey. In all probability, a small group of villagers had access to a number of buckets and perhaps a hand cart to carry a ladder. Maybe a bell was rung to summon the party and they would hurry to the fire. Other people, no doubt, would gather and form a human chain and the water-filled buckets would be passed along the line. All the men were volunteers. The earliest record of a Fire Brigade in the town was *c.*1858.

St Hilary's Fire

Parishioners had complained to Mr John Coventry, the Sexton at St Hilary's Church in January 1857 that the church was very cold on the Sunday morning. He was doing his best but being annoyed he thought "I'll show 'em. It WILL be warm next Sunday".

Now John was a local grocer and had permission to store bacon in the boiler-house. Perhaps he 'smoked' the bacon with the help of oak logs there too. So on the Saturday night 31 January he lit the boiler fire at about eight o'clock and before leaving the church he stoked up the boiler and filled it to the top with fuel. "That will get it hot all right", he muttered to himself as he closed the iron door of the boiler and went home to bed.

The bacon was hanging on hooks from the ceiling and as the boiler got hotter and hotter the fat of the bacon started to melt and dripped onto the top of the hot boiler which soon burst into flames and some old prayer mats caught alight. In a short time the place was on fire and the church was alight.

A villager happened to look through his bedroom window at about two o'clock in the morning when he spotted the flames and smoke rising from the church. He hurried to the rectory to raise the alarm. The Rector and a number of parishioners hurried up the hill and found flames were now breaking through the windows of the church. As there was no Fire Brigade in Wallasey, a messenger was despatched to the nearest fire fighting unit at Birkenhead.

The crowd watched helplessly as the flames spread rapidly, being visible from several miles away. The roof fell in causing sparks to fly into the air. The parishioners could now hear the bell of the Birkenhead Fire Brigade Engine as horses raced down the hill.

They arrived at about 3.30am but by then the church was well alight and the Firemen had difficulty in obtaining water. However, all helped with buckets and the engine was put into action but it was too late to be effective. The church was well and truly ablaze. The floors of the tower caught alight and fell away and the flames were drawn up as in a chimney. The set of six bells crashed down onto the flags below making a great clatter. Only two bells survived the crash, the others being smashed to pieces. The musicians' gallery, organ and pews went up in flames and the building was destroyed, leaving a shell of stone walls and tower standing. The pipe organ had only been installed in church in 1839, costing 300 guineas and replacing the barrel organ of 1826. Other improvements had been made including re-roofing and the new font presented by Mr Chambers at a considerable cost.

It was first thought that the fire had been caused by the overheating of the flues which ignited the flooring and it was said that the Rector, the Reverend Frederick Haggit, had managed to save the Parish Registers and other documents, but in fact it was members of the Coventry family who had risked their lives with the Rector probably assisting them. However, the Sexton was dismissed for causing the fire. The Church was covered by

Keenans Cottage in Mill Lane is where Harry Keenan, the caretaker and holder of the key for the Water Tower, lived. This thatched cottage was demolished c.1912

insurance with the Sun Fire Office to the extent in the region of £2,000.

News of the fire spread quickly and the following day crowds came from all over the district to see the ruins. There had been at least two previous fires at the church as we know this as there is a local saying:-

Thrice burnt
Twice been a church without a tower
and once a tower without a church.

This was the first mention of a serious fire that was attended by the Birkenhead Brigade.

******

School Fire

There used to be a large three-storey house at the foot of Magazine Lane, built in the early 1800s which, by the 1840s was the *Liscard Hotel,* later to become the *New Brighton Hotel* then the *Stanley Arms*. It closed down as a hostelry and Dr Poggi opened the building as a school named New Brighton College. The doctor, who had previously run a school in Seacombe, was a friend of the great Garibaldi, 'the Liberator of Italy', who sent his two sons, Riciotti and Menotti there.

A fire broke out at the school in 1864 which caused a great deal of damage There is no record of a Fire Brigade attending but there could have been as part of the building was saved. This portion was later used as a baker's shop and there was enough room for him to have a flour warehouse. The school continued, Dr Poggi having taken a house near the bottom of Victoria Road, New Brighton (higher up from the *Ferry Hotel*) as a temporary measure. An old rough diary of Menotti was found in the attic of the Victoria Road house in 1880 but there was no mention of the fire at the school. The two boys later returned to their father in Italy.

******

Ship Yard

One of Seacombe's well-known ship building yards, Bowdler and Chaffer (near Seacombe Ferry), suffered a fire on 31 January 1872 which caused £3,000 worth of damageand could have led to their closure in 1877 as the company were just recovering from a strike of shipwrights. They had built several ships in the course of operating from the banks of the Mersey including the famous yacht *Sunbeam* for Lord Brassey in 1874. Lady Brassey wrote a book about her voyages that became a best-seller.

We're sober men and true

WS Gilbert

Wallasey Fire Brigade

The first official Fire Brigade in Wallasey was a volunteer Brigade which started in the 1800s. A Fire Station was established in the front yard of the Liscard Water Tower in Mill Lane. This fine large Water Tower with the tank at the top which held 150,000 gallons, was built in Norman style by Mr Henry Pooley between 1859/61 and opened by Mr Tollemache, MP; it is now a listed building.

Captain WT Leather was in charge of the outdoor water department and once lived in Liscard Crescent. He would go out at night and make soundings for water bursts. He was appointed Wallasey's first Fire Chief and wore a uniform with brass helmet. In the 1870s their equipment consisted of no more than a hand-cart, a few ladders, a leather hose-reel, stand pipes, keys and bars, buckets and, later, a 40ft. Escape. There were about six or seven Auxiliaries who were connected with water in one way or another, being plumbers or employed in the building trade. Their knowledge of water mains and pipes was invaluable.

By all accounts, the fire appliance was a hand-drawn cart. Possibly with a centre shaft for two strong men either side to haul it along. It must have had a pump and hose-reel, hence it was known as 'The Reel'. The cart would have had either two or four wheels.

The Fire Bell was hung at the top of the tower with a stout rope attached. When sounded the Firemen would come running to the yard in Mill Lane. There was a cry of "Fire!" and the locals would gather outside the water tower.

The Firemen rushed into the yard and hauled out the reel from the shed and two Firemen would get between the shaft of the appliance. Firemen would climb on the reel and a long rope of about 40 feet was tied to the shaft for other Firemen and helpers, who had rallied around to help, to pull the appliance to the scene of the fire. They would pick other Firemen as the hurried along the streets.

And a right good captain, too!
You're all very good,
And be it understood,
I command a right good crew.

WS Gilbert

Early volunteer Firemen under Captain Leather were John Bleakley, Robert Carson, John Dutton, John Fellowes, Harold Gibbons, James Lea and Thomas Somerville. Harold Gibbons, was no doubt, the son of Stephen Gibbons the coach proprietor of Liscard Village. Most Saturday afternoons in the summer, the Firemen would practice. The bell would be rung and the men would rush out and connect up their equipment to the water supply. They enjoyed the exercise as much as did the local children who had gathered to watch the proceedings. On one occasion they were practising outside the Nelson Hotel. John Bleakley was squirting water from the hose across the road. Some of the locals heard the noise and came to the door of the pub holding their pints of ale. They watched the procedure and started to pass some comments which caused laughter. Bleakley now had the nozzle pointing upwards, with the water squirting to a fair height which caused the locals to shout some rude remarks. Captain Leather leant to one side and said in a low tone "Let them have it, Jack." Bleakley turned the nozzle a degree or so and the water poured down on the noisy element with some of them losing the ale from their glasses only to see a little clear water in the bottom. They were so surprised at the loss of the beer, that they were not completely aware of being

The first Fire Station in Wallasey was established in the front yard of the Liscard Water Tower, seen here in Mill Lane. St Alban's Church is seen in the background

drenched.

The Firemen had the last laugh!

One Sunday lunchtime the Fire Brigade attended a blaze at William Clarke's paint shop in Victoria Road, Seacombe (now Borough Road). The fire was in the attic and John Bleakley was told to take the hose and play the water on the flames, followed by another Fireman to ease the weight of the hose. Bleakley looked down and called "come and hold the nozzle" The Fireman swung the nozzle around and turned to answer the call from Bleakley below. Police Inspector Hindley, who had arrived on the scene, went into the house only to be met with the full force of the jet which knocked him off his feet backwards. The drenched Inspector picked himself up and shouted at the Fireman "who gave you permission to come up here?" "No one", replied the innocent Fireman. "Then get down at once" roared the Inspector. The fire was soon extinguished and although the Inspector had a good soaking, these two men became great friends.

*****

The Battle of the Brickworks

The Egremont Brickworks which were near the river on a site between what is now Tobin Street and Maddock Road, exported their bricks all over the world. In most cases, the bricks were loaded from the sea wall onto lighters. This wall ran along the front that had been constructed by the Mersey Docks and Harbour Board and was completed in 1863. The top of the wall was about a yard in width and people would walk along it. There were no railings and one had to be careful when the tide was rough. The path eventually became a right of way. The brickwork people used to load up the flats at high water as they moored against the wall. Passers-by would stand and watch the procedure. The management thought that one day someone could have an accident so they constructed a wooden fence in the December of 1877 to stop people walking along the top of the wall. The Local Board did not approve so the Chairman of the

Works Committee, Mr Henry Skinner, decided to take action. The Fire Brigade, under the supervision of Captain WT Leather, was asked to remove it. The barrier was knocked down and thrown into the river but the Brickwork management got their men to replace it. The Brigade were told to go down again and remove it. This was done and the timber thrown into the river once more. Another was built but this time it was much stouter and the beams had a railing on top with iron spikes.

A small crowd had gathered on the Saturday at Egremont Ferry to see what would happen. The Fire Brigade arrived to a cheer and the Police were present together with a gang of men from the brickworks, who were not happy with the brick-making machines that had been introduced. By now it was high tide and the Firemen attacked the heavy barrier with axes from the other side of the barrier. The brickworkers tried to push two brothers, Bill and Jim Carney, into the water with long poles as they attempted to help the Firemen in their task. They were knocked off and one fell into the water and had to be hauled out. The Firemen then produced some heavy saws and started to saw through the beams.

The brickwork men had laid a hose pipe from the boiler house down to the sea wall and drilled holes in the end section so the hot water would spray those attempting to dismantle the barrier. They also dug a three foot pit and filled it with puddled clay, covering it with loose earth. As the hot water sprayed on the Firemen, they retreated and some of them fell in the pit as bricks were hurled at them from the other side of the fence.

It was now that the Police decided to act. Enough was enough. Under the command of Inspector Hindley, they raided the works and arrested two of the directors and a few workmen for hurling bricks at the Firemen and soon the battle was over. They appeared in court and the matter was settled. The public would have the right of way. One of the directors that had been arrested, was Thomas Valentine Burrows who was later elected to the Urban District Council in 1891, became a Justice of the Peace in 1904 and Chairman of the Council. In 1910, he was made an Alderman of the Wallasey Council and was elected Mayor of Wallasey for 1913/14.

The Egremont Brickworks had a life of some 15 years before the

This was first official photograph of the full Wallasey Fire Brigade and was taken outside Cliff House, Mariners' Park, Egremont. The Chief and all the Firemen with the two Fire Engines are assembled. Two Wheeled Escapes are raised up to the balcony with four men on each. Two Sergeants stand by the horses, with Firemen, who can be seen wearing brass helmets and axes in their belts, taking up their places on each Engine and a small group in front of the main door.

company went into the building trade operating from their office and yard in King Street, building many houses in the town just before the turn of the century.

The sea wall was a dangerous place to walk along with one person losing his life. This led to railings being erected and eventually the promenade was constructed behind it in 1891.

******

Horse-Drawn Fire Engines

And a milk-white horse,
As a matter of course.

WS Gilbert

It is not known when Wallasey first had a Horse-Drawn Fire Engine but the Brigade took command of a Horse-Drawn Manual Pump with a four-wheeled carriage that was pulled by two horses supplied by Gibbons' Stables of Liscard, which later became the site of the old Capitol Cinema in 1926 (*see picture opposite*). Stephen Gibbons also had stables opposite the old *Boot Inn* in Wallasey Road. Fireman John Bushell, the Liscard Road butcher, became the driver of the Engine.

Arthur Leather, possibly related to the Captain, became their vet. Early Fire Engines were paid for by public subscription.

The Brigade had about eight volunteer Firemen under the command of Captain Leather. They wore a navy blue uniform with six metal buttons either side, long boots and a cloth sailor-type hat. They also had the brass helmet for firefighting. They did not wear collar and ties, but like the policemen, the collar fastened at the neck. Messrs. Merryweather was the main supplier of helmets and other items.

Up until then, the Fire Engine was still left at the Tower Yard in Mill Lane. However, there was a drawback with this arrangement. The only holder of the key was Harry Keenan, the caretaker of the Water Tower, who lived in Tower Cottage, later known as Granny Smith's, a single storey white-washed cottage that stood on the corner of what is now Dinmore Road. If he or his wife, Ellan, were out, there would be a problem (*see picture on page 6*).

Meanwhile, two men fetched the horses to Mill Lane and the first Fireman to arrive would toll the bell on top of the tower to summon the rest of the men.

There was a fire at the Palace, New Brighton on Easter Saturday 1881 which burnt down the skating rink, which had opened the day before. It is not known who fought the flames and brought the fire under control. Some folk were not happy with it being opened on the holy day and thought it was because of this it had suffered the fire.

And the wicked flames may hiss

WS Gilbert

The Fire Brigade Report of 1891 stated that during the year the Liscard Fire Brigade attended six fires and Seacombe Fire Branch four.

On the 3 March they were called out at 9.10am to a chimney fire at a house in Victoria Road in New Brighton which was occupied by Mr E Laybourne. It took two hours to put out and caused £100 worth of damage.

The Brigade was called out at 9.05am on 28 March to attend a fire that had broken out on board the SS *City of New York* at Alfred Dock. It was three hours before the Fireman left the ship.

A chimney fire brought the Brigade into action at Noon on 8 June at Mr Frank Pooley's home *Homecroft,* Manor Road. The Firemen were there for two hours and it caused £20 worth of damage.

Built in 1848 by his grandfather, Henry Pooley the Iron Founder, this fine mansion had a magnificent archway of King William Pear Trees with a drive leading to the front entrance. There was also a coach-house and stables to the east of the building. Henry Pooley and Son's patent weighing machines were seen on all railway stations throughout the country. They also manufactured weighbridges and had their iron works, the Albion Foundry, in

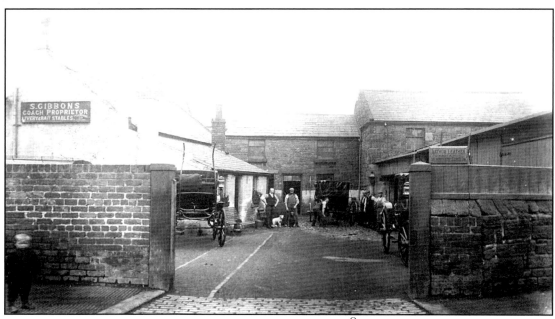

Gibbon's Stables in Liscard supplied the horses for the Fire Brigade.

The Fire Station was later built opposite his premises and they would stable their horses with him.

The old Capitol Cinema *in Wallasey Village was developed on the site in 1926*

Liverpool where they employed some 700 men and boys. Mr. Pooley gave the parish a number of drinking fountains placed throughout the district.

There was a call-out to Mr J Bailey's stables in Victoria Road, New Brighton at 10.15am on 15 July. Started by sparks from an adjoining chimney, it took five hours to put out and clean up. The fire caused £150 worth of damage.

The Brigade were called out at 10.30am on 7 October to put out a burning haystack at Mr Nicoll's Manor Farm. The Brigade were at the scene for three hours with damage estimated at £5.

On 16 October the Fire Brigade was called out at 2.30pm to deal with an overheated stove at Mr. Andrews' *Stanley Arms Hotel* in Victoria Road, Seacombe. They were there three hours and £10 worth of damage was inflicted.

In November the Brigade was called out at 5.15am to a fire at GH Lowry's baker's shop in Rake Lane and were there for six hours. There was £600 worth of damage caused.

The alarm was raised from Mr Jones at Victoria Road, Seacombe on 10 December where sparks from the adjoining property caused a small fire in his stack yard. Only £1 worth of damage was done to Mr. Jones' property and the Brigade had it all cleared up in an hour.

A second manual Fire Engine was added to the Brigade at this time and they also had two Wheeled Escapes which could be carried by either Engine. It is said that hose carts were kept in sheds in Seacombe and Wallasey Village.

> When the red sheet winds and whirls
> In coil of frightful death;
> When the banner'd smoke unfurls,
> And the hot walls drink our breath;
> When the far-off crowd appears
> Choking in the demon glare,
> And some helpless form appears
> In that furnace of despair:–
> "Save, Oh, Save!" the people cry:
> But who plucks the human brand?
> Who will do the deed or die?
> 'Tis a fireman of the land.
> Then give them honour, give them fame!
> A health to hands that fight the flame!
>
> **A 19th Century Poem by E.Cook**

Fire Stations in Wallasey

It was suggested that owing to the alarming proportions of one of the fires at New Brighton, a Branch Brigade should be established in that part of the town. This suggestion was at once adopted by the Health Committee, members were enrolled and arrangements made for their equipment with a small Station being set up in the Albert Hall (later to become the site of the *Trocadero Picture House*) in Victoria Road.

A local Fire Station

Firemen are standing in front of Manor Road Fire Station which was opened in Liscard, replacing the one in Mill Lane. This one was demolished in August 1914 to make way for the new one

Thirty Firemen and Officers are assembled in Central Park, Liscard. The men are wearing new black leather helmets that had two brass bands around the brim for reflection. Their tunics are three-quarter length. The Fire Chief and other officials are standing in front of the new Horse-Drawn Steamer and the two other Horse-Drawn Fire Engines.

It was also decided that the Fire Station in Mill Lane should be taken down and a new one built on the Board's Yard adjoining the Public Weighing Machine at the Liscard Village end of Manor Road . The site had been given by a local gentleman.

Work started in Manor Road (which was later to become the site of the Fire Station Duty Room after the Second World War) and a building erected to house the Horse-Drawn Manual Pump next to the stables and Public Weigh-Bridge. These buildings were converted into a two storey stable with a duty room and drill yard at the rear and a new house for the Steamer. A gas lamp was placed above the tall doors that had the word 'Fire' on the dark glass which showed up at night. The original alarm bell from Mill Lane Water Tower, was taken down and re-fixed in the turret of the new two-storey Station. The front of the building was cobbled-stoned and was a small island in the middle of the road with a drinking fountain, which was used by the horses that pulled the tramcars, topped with a tall lamp-post. It was also the place where the horses were changed. It was from here in the 1920s that the supporters of New Brighton Football Club, who were in the Third Division North, would take the short tram journey up Rake Lane to Sandheys Park.

The keeper of the Public Weighing Machine was a man by the name Enoch H Spragg.

The Central Fire Station in Liscard Village was duly opened in 1898. Cox's Slaughter House was behind the Fire Station yard and where sheep or cattle could be seen driven into the yard to await slaughter. This was the same family who later ran a motor coach business in Wallasey.

In the 1890s, Wallasey had two Horse-Drawn Pumps that were hauled by two horses with enough room for three Firemen to stand on either side of the Engine in addition to the driver. The horses were kept at Gibbons' Stables and when the Fire Alarm Bell was rung at the Station, the horses would gallop across the field and put their necks over the gate and wait for the Firemen to take them across to the Station. The horse collar went around its neck clipped at the top-thus saving time. All the horse-drawn vehicles had the single shaft, with a horse on either side.

In 1898, the Wallasey Urban District Council took over the responsibility of the Fire Brigade and the men then received a small retaining fee, thus ended the Voluntary Fire Brigade.

It became necessary to have other branches in the town. A Sub-Station was set up in Brighton Street under or next to John Howarth, a tobacconist who was Volunteer Fireman, and another branch in Wallasey Village under the Water Inspector, Abraham Halewood. The fire cart and equipment was kept in a building next to the

Wallasey Public Weigh Bridge in Leasowe Road. It was known as the Wallasey Fire Station.

The original Horse-Drawn Pump was used for many years and was last used at the New Brighton Tower fire in 1898.

Oh! joy, our Chief is saved

WS Gilbert

The Brigade had been called to the docks where a ship had caught fire. The Firemen went aboard and were fighting the blaze when Fireman John Dutton saw another Firemen fall from the ship into the dock and seeing a bald head floating just below the surface of the water, hauled the unfortunate Fireman out. It turned out to be Captain Leather who had been saved due to the fact that he was bald and had lost his brass helmet! There were nine Auxiliaries who would run to the Central Fire Station when the bell was rung (the bell was later used in Central Park to signal closing time). Next to the Fire Station was the old *Blue Bell Inn* which was demolished in 1899.

The Firemen wore the brass helmet donning the badge consisting of two crossed axes over a flaming torch which was also used by other Brigades but the Fire Chiefs in some Brigades wore a silver helmet which would stand out especially at a fire. Senior Officers today wear a white helmet.

The early Horse-Drawn Fire Engines were painted black and usually hauled by a pair of horses but it was not until 1914 that the people of Wallasey saw a 'Red Fire Engine'.

In the early days, it was not uncommon to see the Firemen with full beards and a good number had large moustaches.

The Brigade was now under the command of Superintendent John Howarth, who had taken over from Captain Leather.

On 3 February 1895 there was a fire at the Congregational Church, Liscard Road which was dealt with by the Brigade.

Buchanan's Flour Mills on the East Float caught fire on 5 July 1895 but was saved by the prompt action of the Brigade.

On 28 March the following year there was a fire in the heating apparatus chamber at St James' Church, New Brighton which spread to the tower. The Fire Brigade was summoned and promptly extinguished the flames without further damage.

The Fire Brigade took great pride in the May Day Parades from the 1890s and into the 1900s when they decorated the engine on parade with coloured silks and flowers. The Horse-Drawn Fire Engine turned out in 1894, being hauled by two horses, one black and the other white. In the 1898 May Day Parade, they used two black horses.

For the 1900 May Day Parade, the Fire Brigade used a Fire Engine with two white horses. The Firemen wore the sailor type soft hats. In another May Day Parade, the Firemen donned their polished brass helmets. Some were given a new hank of rope which they attached to their belts. The Fire Brigade also took part in the popular Wallasey Village Festival Parades.

The following lines were written at the time about the many photographers who took their wonderful pictures.

Then all the crowd take down our looks
In pocket memorandum books.
To diagnose
Our modest pose
The Kodaks do their best
If evidence you would possess
Of what is manly bashfulness,
You only need a button press -
And we do the rest.

WS Gilbert

The First New Brighton Tower Fire

In 1898, the New Brighton Tower grounds had just opened but the builders were still working on the higher portion of the tower structure. In order to protect the crowds below, they had placed wooden planks around part of the building to prevent injury from falling bricks etc.

Shortly after 10pm on 1 April 1898 a Call-Out was received and the Wallasey Fire Brigade rushed to the scene to find that the wooden planks 172ft. up were ablaze. Their Manual Pump was not powerful enough to reach that height so the Birkenhead and Liverpool Fire Brigades were asked to attend with their Steam Pumps.

Both Brigades agreed to come but Birkenhead had to obtain permission from the Council to leave their Borough whilst Liverpool had to wait until a Luggage Boat got steam up. Meanwhile the Wallasey Firemen showed great courage by climbing onto the planks to fight the flames.

Unfortunately a young Volunteer Fireman, Jim Shone, a bricksetter from Seacombe, lost his footing while attempting to reach the blaze and fell 90 feet to his death.

It was not until midnight that the other Brigades arrived by which time the fire had burnt itself out.

Following the death on duty of the Wallasey Fireman, measures were taken to improve the Fire Service. It was decided that the Manual Pump would have to be replaced by a modern Engine and an order was placed for a new Shand Mason Horse-Drawn Steamer.

******

We spectres are a jollier crew
Than you, perhaps, suppose!

WS Gilbert

Humour

The Firemen have always had a good sense of humour and over the years they had many funny stories to relate. Nevertheless they took firefighting very seriously and would risk their lives to save life whenever necessary. The same applies to the Firefighters of today.

On one occasion, the Brigade were called to a fire in New Brighton, and there was a slight delay in leaving the Fire Station. While they were on their way, a certain Mr. Alltree was standing at his door. He was somewhat amused and shouted out to the Firemen:

"The fire will be out the time you get there!"

It was strange that he should have made such a sarcastic remark, for later that day his own place caught fire and he was glad of their service as they had managed to stop the fire from burning his premises down. The Firemen always reminded him about it and as a member of the Local Board he fought to get the Brigade a better Engine.

The Steamer

Instead of the Shand Mason engine originally ordered, the Brigade purchased a Merryweather 360gpm Horse-Drawn Steamer on 17 December 1898 with financial help from an anonymous benefactor. It had a brightly polished boiler at the rear for heating the water which would be lit as soon as they left the Fire Station. A Fireman would stoke up the boiler and with the pressure building, by the time they reached the fire there was sufficient power to operate the single-action pump. It worked on the same principal as the old donkey-engine, the steam working the piston cylinder. The four wheels of the vehicle were very stout, with the larger pair at the rear. The Steamer was named after Councillor Dr TWA Napier, MD, JP, who was Honorary Captain of the Brigade (the doctor retired from the Council in 1907) and the words 'Wallasey Urban District Council' were on the side; his name was in front of the driver's foot rest.

The Fire Engine, which would normally be hauled by two horses or sometimes four, was housed at Manor Road Fire Station where an engineer, Ernest Platt, was employed.

The public were able to get a good view of the new Fire Steam Engine when it was proudly hauled by four horses along Brighton Street in the May Day Parade.

The Wallasey Fire Brigade now had the Steamer and the two Horse-drawn Pumps one of which was kept at the Seacombe Fire Station and the horses were still kept at Gibbons' Stables across the road.

Chemical Engine

The Wallasey Fire Brigade, with the help of a local gentleman and others, took charge of a 60 gallon Merryweather Horse-Drawn Chemical Engine/Escape in 1900. This Fire Engine worked on the same principal as a fire-extinguisher. A very large copper cylinder

Superintendent John Howarth poses with his staff on the Steamer

11

*Boys of the Old Brigade with the Steam Engine
decorated for the May Day Parade*

was mounted at the rear of an ordinary Fire Engine which held 60 gallons of water. Sodium bicarbonate was then dissolved in it. Above the cylinder was another container which held sulphuric acid. When the Fireman operated a wheel-valve it punctured the top of the container which allowed the acid to shoot into the copper cylinder. The two chemicals then reacted and formed carbon dioxide gas. This drove the water out at about 100 lb/inch pressure. Once the top container had been punctured, there was no way in which to stop the water until the full 60 gallons had been used. When more water was needed, additional hoses had to supply it from a Manual Pump Engine. Later Chemical Engines had improvements with an extra bottle of acid; others with a tank of compressed air.

It was always a great sight to see the Fire Engine racing along the streets and hear the bell ringing and clatter of the horses' hooves on the cobblestones. People would hurry after them to see where the fire was. At this time the Brigade had the steamer, the chemical engine, a horse carriage and two escapes.

The Fire Brigade was also responsible for the Ambulance Service, which had started with a simple hand-propelled stretcher. This was made to be clipped onto a two-wheeled carriage with four legs on hinges that could be turned down to keep it steady while the stretcher was attached. The end of the stretcher could be raised for the patient's head and four rods could be added to support a cover, if necessary. The Horse-Drawn Ambulance, which had previously operated from Gibbons' Stables was now kept at the Fire Station.

The Seacombe Sub-Station was in Platt Street where a manual engine was operated by six Auxiliaries under the command of Sgt. William Clark. Messrs. Kenna, the funeral directors, supplied the horses.

The Wallasey Horse-drawn Fire Engine races to the fire

Six Auxiliaries were in charge of the red-painted, Hand-Drawn Hose Cart at Folly Gutt in Wallasey Village and there was a similar cart on hand at New Brighton which was kept in Egerton Street with five Auxiliaries available and Sergeant Joseph Dodd in charge. In most cases these Fire Carts carried a ladder, brass squirts and canvas buckets. The ladder enabled the men rescue people from the first floor windows. With better water mains in the town, these carts eventually carried a hydrant standpipe and canvas hose.

Big Fire

On Saturday night 20 October 1900 there was a serious fire at the Seacombe works of Messrs. Currie, Rowlands & Co., the cattle food manufacturers on the Dock Road.

The factory was closed as usual on Saturday afternoon but at 10pm a man working in one of the neighbouring premises spotted the flames coming from the cattle food factory and immediately called the Fire Brigade.

Superintendent Howarth turned out from the Central Fire Station in Liscard with a crew on the Chemical Engine. On arriving , he saw that there was no hope of saving the building and directed all efforts toward preventing the spread of the fire to the neighbouring premises. The firemen worked their hardest at great personal risk and it was six o'clock on Sunday morning before the Superintendent deemed it safe to hand over the premises to the care of the Liverpool Salvage Corps. Practically all the machinery and stock was destroyed.

Mr. Abraham Halewood

Abraham Halewood lived in a cottage at 51, Wallasey Village that was between Buxton House and Olive Farm. Being a Water Inspector it was only natural that he should be appointed Sergeant-in-Charge of the Local Volunteer Fire Brigade. They dressed in a standard dark blue uniform with brass helmets and had to pull the Fire Cart, which was kept in Folly Lane by what became Thomas' Farm, to any fire in the village.

Often the gorse would catch alight and they would put it out by beating the flames; hay stacks would catch fire by combustion and Firemen could be seen racing across the fields carrying buckets of water.

Abraham was Secretary of the Wallasey Workmens' Club in St George's Road and gave Yeoman service to the community and

William Liversage, an early Volunteer Fireman at New Brighton Sub-Station, was also a member of the New Brighton Lifeboat crew

was also Church Warden at St Hilary's Church. His son, David, was a market gardener. Abraham Halewood died on 19 March 1917 aged 70 years. His wife, Abigail, died on 1 September 1920 aged 74 years.

******

Uniform

The Firemen's double-breasted tunic of Melton cloth had two rows of metal buttons either side which fastened to the neck, being modelled on the 'Lancer' style of jacket. There were two polished brass buttons on the back that reflected light from the flames so that other Firemen were able to see them in the dark. The same applied to the epaulettes. The wide leather belt carried a large metal buckle and a hustler for the bright axe. Their trousers were placed over their boots so that when they pulled them on all they had to do was slip their feet into their heavy leather jack boots sometimes called 'Cotton Oxfords' and put their fingers into the tabs. They were supplied by Pocock Brothers at 55 shillings a pair.

The Firemen wore a brass polished helmet for head protection but it also served as a reflector at night. It was discontinued when electricity became popular for fear of the men getting an electric shock when the helmet came into contact with overhead live wires. This was followed by the hard helmet that had two brass bands running around it. The helmet badge consisted of two crossed fire axes and flaming torch of the older pattern. At a later date it had the town's Coat of Arms in the centre.

The helmet also saved the men from moulted lead that often fell from the old lead gas and water pipes that melted with the heat of the fire.

Mr. William Liversage

One of earliest Volunteer Firemen at New Brighton Sub-Station was that of William James Liversage (1864-1923) who was born in a house next to the *Ferry Hotel,* New Brighton, being the son of Samuel and Jane Liversage. William became a well-known character in the resort and was appointed New Brighton Pier Master *c.*1900 and in addition to being a Volunteer Fireman he was also a member of the New Brighton Lifeboat. He was a Lifeboatman on board the *William and Kate Johnson* that went to the assistance of the French steamer *Emilie Delmas* which had started to drag her anchors four miles of the Bar Lightship at 7am on 24 November 1928. A fierce gale was blowing with gusts of 100mph. The Lifeboat put to sea 45 minutes later with a full crew. With great skill, Coxswain Robinson managed to draw along side the stricken vessel taking off 23 members of her crew, the Captain being last to leave the ship. The damaged Lifeboat drew away and headed back to New Brighton. However, a huge wave swept two members of the crew and the Chief Engineer of the French steamer overboard. The Coxswain Robinson, with difficulty, turned the Lifeboat around and managed to pick up George Carmody and Sam Jones. Sadly, the Chief Engineer was drowned.

Coxswain George Robinson was awarded the RNLI's Silver Medal for his gallantry and Bronze Medals to the rest of the crew.

The owners of the *Emilie Delmas* were so impressed that they gave 10,000 francs to the members of the Lifeboat crew and the French Government presented gold medals to the Coxswain and Lifeboatmen Carmody and Jones.

Mr. Liversage was a Bowman for seventeen and a half years with the New Brighton Lifeboat. Framed Testimonials to him can be seen in the Lifeboat House in New Brighton.

Mr. Liversage also performed three rescues independently of the Lifeboat Service for which he received the Royal Humane Society's Medal with two Bars.

In 1914, William Liversage went to the aid of 37 year-old Amy Williams of Seabank Road who had fallen from the ferryboat *John Joyce.* Without hesitation, he dived in the water and rescued her. A year later, he saved Nellie White of Albion Street who had attempted to commit suicide. He had been digging for bait at

The Fire Brigade were called to this fire at 154 Victoria Road, Seacombe next to Devine Bros. grocery stores on 29 May 1906

Harrison Drive at the time.

In 1919, William Liversage was going to Liverpool on business when he happened to see eight-year-old Albert Hughes of 36 Wilton Street, Liverpool, fall into the water from the back of the Landing Stage. Again he went into action and saved the child. Mr. Liversage died on 3 December 1923 aged 59.

******

Horses

Horses, as previously mentioned, were hired from Gibbons' Livery Stables but in 1906, it was decided that the Brigade should have their own horses. Three suitable horses were purchased and a stable was built at Gibbons' Yard opposite the Fire Station, as there were no full-time men, other than the Superintendent and Engineer, to look after the animals and to clean out the stables. The stables at the Fire Station were used for other purposes, maybe to house the Ambulance.

On 20 October 1900 there was a great fire at the Oil Mills, Seacombe and the Brigade went into action once more but little could be done to save the building.

There was a Call-Out to a fire at 154 Victoria Road, Seacombe on 29 May 1906. Smoke bellowed through the window above the shop. Mrs. Sandeman, whose husband had the shop beneath, came to the window and called for help. Someone went and borrowed a window cleaner's ladder and Mrs Sandeman was rescued from the first floor window. Meanwhile, two volunteers raced to the Fire Station in Brougham Road, and got the horse from the stable which pulled the Pump to the fire where they were able to stop the fire from spreading next door to Devine Brothers grocery stores.

The Brougham Road Fire Station was near the Guinea Gap bend of the road leading into Demesne Street. It was a lock-up building with tiled walls and folding doors for ease and speed of opening. Originally, there was only a hand-cart at the Station. The key was held by Superintendent John Howarth, the Chief Fire Officer, and operated by volunteers who were not on the premises.

Superintendent John Howarth died on 17 January 1902 aged 58 years and was buried in Rake Lane Cemetery. His wife, Margaret

Parkin, died on 9 January, 1915 aged 72 years. Mr GW Byne became the new Superintendent and Chief Fire Officer.

On 19 December 1908 there was a fire at the *Irving Theatre* in Seacombe. The Brigade was called and fought the blaze which caused well over £1,000 worth of damage to the scenery, instruments and building. Luckily, the scenery for the pantomime 'Aladdin' was virtually untouched and the show was moved to the New Brighton Tower Theatre.

The theatre closed for a considerable time while renovations and repairs were carried out.

Ironically, this theatre had staged a play called 'Still Alarm' a week before the fire. A real Fire Engine and horses were on the stage and a copy of the Central Fire Station in New York City erected.

There was one occasion when the Brigade was called to a fire in Victoria Road. Two Engines raced to Seacombe but on arrival discovered that the fire was in Victoria Road, New Brighton! They had to turn around and gallop off again. The horses must have been exhausted by the time they got to the fire and valuable time had been lost. After this occurance, the Victoria Road in Seacombe changed its name to Borough Road.

A large bang was heard in New Brighton in 1909 which brought people to their front doors. It was the result of an explosion in the boiler room at St James' Church in Albion Street which fractured the gas main. Luckily no one was injured. The church suffered damage to the organ with some of the organ pipes being blown through the church windows and onto the roofs of nearby houses. Also Several houses, including the Vicarage, had their windows broken by the blast.

By 1909 some of Firemen were employed full-time as the horses had to be looked after and exercised, the new stables cleaned out and the Engines had to be maintained.

The Wallasey Village Sub-Station, with its hose and ladder cart, was operated by Sergeant Halewood.

The smoke hoods were modernised in the 1900s with oxygen cylinders self-breathing apparatus becoming popular with Brigades.

Wallasey became a Borough in 1910, its Charter was the first to be

Superintendent GW Byne is pictured on the right in all his regalia together with his men on the Mayor's Sunday Parade who all look resplendent in their uniform with brass helmets, in Wallasey in 1911

*Mill Lane Hospital forInfectious Diseases was opened in 1887
(see previous page for details)*

granted by King George V. The first Council consisted of 10 Aldermen and 30 Councillors who met on 11 November 1910. They invited Mr James Thomas Chester, who was not a Councillor, to be Mayor. By now the Fire Brigade had a Superintendent, an Engineer and six full-time Firemen. Land had been purchased next to the Fire Station in Manor Road in 1910 and a loan sanction was later obtained for the building of a larger purpose-built Fire Station and Superintendent's house; also two Dennis Motor Engines.

There was a Call-Out to a fire aboard the Bibby Liner SS *Warwickshire* that was at berth in the Alfred Dock, Seacombe, June 1911. This was a difficult fire to deal with and Sergeant Peter Leather, Firemen W Davies, Bob Herron, D Campbell and John Walker all suffered injuries which required hospital treatment.

The Brigade would be often called out to deal with Chimney fires being caused by not having them swept on a regular basis. Some people would deliberately set their chimneys on fire to save having them swept. George Whitman and Eliza Brown both appeared before the Magistrates' Court in 1912 on separate charges of neglecting to sweep their chimneys. They were fined six pence each and four shillings and six pence costs for allowing them to catch fire.

******

Council takes over

The Wallasey Borough Council took responsibility of the Brigade in 1912. Full-time Superintendent GW Byne was in charge and he now had a full-time staff of eight Firemen and an Engineer. In addition, he could call on an Auxiliary Sergeant and a further seven men. It seems soon after the number of Auxiliaries increased to 14 men and two Sergeants.

Mr Byne lived at 7 Manor Road and Police Sergeant Joseph D Venables at No.23. Mr & Mrs Byne later went to live at 8 Anglesey Road.

At No.1 Central Fire Station, Manor Road there was a Horse-Drawn Steamer, Horse-Drawn Chemical Escape, a Hand-Drawn Hose (Tender) and Ladder Truck. They also had a Hose Truck and a Hand-Drawn 40ft. Escape and the Horse-Drawn Ambulance. When the Victoria Central Hospital in Liscard Road opened on 1 January 1901, the New Brighton Tower Company donated a new Horse-Drawn Ambulance and this was probably the one kept at the Fire Station.

In about 1890, Dr Bouverie and FP MacDonald, had presented Seacombe Cottage Hospital with a Horse-Drawn Ambulance Wagon. This was kept at Seacombe and when that hospital closed 31 January 1901 it was then moved to the Fire Station in Manor Road. The Horses were stabled at Gibbons' in Liscard Village.

The Seacombe Dispensary for Children had been established in Fell Street (opened 1 January 1867) and later in 1871, a new hospital

was opened at 53 Demesne Street. North Meade House (now the site of the Town Hall) was also used as a hospital for infectious diseases and from 1866 there had been a cottage hospital in Wallasey Village, firstly in Byron Cottage, Back Lane then in Claremount Road. The one in Back Lane (now St George's Road) had been founded in 1866 and the other was opened in 1886.

Mill Lane Hospital for Infectious Diseases was opened in 1887 (*see picture above*).

'Highfield House' had been purchased from the Reece family in 1919 and was the town's first Maternity Hospital which was opened in 1921.

There was a Fever Hospital off Leasowe Road near the bend by the clay pit, with eight beds that had been established in 1902 and was used for smallpox cases. An old grey Ambulance with a canvas top was used for the fever cases. This vehicle could either have been used in the First World War or the motorcar that Dr McDonald had given to the Fire Brigade in 1915 and was converted into an Ambulance Wagon.

No.2 Sub-Station was at Brougham Road, which had been established some years earlier being known as Seacombe Fire Station, there was collection of Pompier Ladders, a Hand-Drawn Hose, Ladder Truck and a 60ft. Hand-Drawn Escape. A Full-Time Fireman was at the Station and there were four Auxiliary Firemen on call.

No.3 substation at Wallasey Village was still manned by three Auxiliary Fireman under the command of Sergeant Halewood. They had a Hose and Ladder Truck.

A 50ft. Hand-Drawn Escape was kept in Albion Street which could be quickly wheeled to any of the large three storey houses or hotels in the area.

The Superintendent, the Engineer and six Firemen held the St John Ambulance First Aid Certificate.

In addition to the mobile Appliances, the Brigade was equipped with six scaling ladders and some 2,000 yards of canvas hose with instantaneous couplings. They had Pompier Belts and five 3.5 gallon chemical extinguishers. The Brigade also had various water tools, branches, life lines, axes and other useful items.

Up to this date, there were no modern smoke helmets.

Early hoses were sewn along the seams and had metal screw connectors. The old leather hoses were heavy and had to be greased periodically to stop them from cracking. The Firemen disliked them as they were very slippery to handle. Later, flax hoses were used.

Never mind the why and wherefore
WS Gilbert

By 1912 the Brigade dealt with 46 non-serious calls including 13 False Alarms, of which four were by telephone, eight by street alarms and one Test Call by the Committee. The Steamer was not in use during the year but nevertheless was regularly and satisfactorily tested in the Station yard with fires being extinguished by the Chemical Engine and hydrants. The Ambulance had been called out to 170 Accidents, of which 156 cases were transported to the hospital and fourteen had received First Aid at home. The Ambulance had also removed 196 of which 152 were conveyed to the Victoria Central Hospital in Liscard Road; 24 to the Cottage Hospital and two to the Southern Hospital in Liverpool. Nine were taken to Nursing Homes and nine were taken home from the Victoria Central Hospital.

The men also took maternity cases to hospital. In addition to the Ambulance work, the men were Firemen. They could come in wet from a big fire, the bells would go down and they would have to go out with the Ambulance. There was 'no knocking off' time in those days.

In 1912, Mrs Porter of 75 Union Street in Egremont paid five shillings for use of the Horse-drawn Ambulance. The Council refunded her money.

The old Water Tower caretaker's cottage in Mill Lane was demolished about 1912 when the road was widened. The last resident living there was Peter Smith. Several photographs of the old cottage still exist, including one of it being re-thatched.

The Post Office looked after the ten Alarm Call Points and handed over the two in Albion Street and Grove Road in November 1912. The Council agreed on 9 December 1912 to the proposal that the Fire Alarm Posts should carry a notice warning people of a penalty of not exceeding £20 for False Alarms.

The town received its County Borough status on 1 April 1913 and in that year the Council approved 'that the subscription of Superintendent Byne amounting to £1.1s.0d to the Fire Brigade Association' to be paid.

The Wallasey Borough Council was responsible for the Brigade. They were represented by:-

HW Cook, Town Clerk.

TWA Napier, MD, JP- Honorary Captain.

WH Travers, AMICE Borough Engineer.

The duty of the Watch Committee was 'to have control and management of the Fire Brigade' with the Chief Constable as Chief Officer.

The Personnel was the same as in 1912, namely, the full-time staff consisting of the Superintendent, an Engineer and eight Firemen. In addition, there were an Auxiliary staff of two Sergeants and 14 Firemen. The average age being 32 years.

The Brigade owned three fine horses.

There were 57 call-out in 1913. It was therefore necessary to increase the number of Firemen.

Superintendent GW Byne attended a congress at Barrow-in-Furness on 2nd and 3rd July 1914 and was allowed £2.3s.10d expenses.

The Council decided that the old Weighing Machine by the Fire Station would be discontinued from October 1913.

Motor Engines and the arrival of Mr Nicholson

I have lived hitherto
Free from breath of slander,
Beloved by all my crew-
A really popular Commander.

WS Gilbert

In 1912, the Council had realised that the growing town should move with the times and have a modern Motor Fire Engine like other authorities.

Mr Barry, the Chief Constable, saw it would also be necessary that the Brigade would have to have a man who had experience with motor vehicles as the men were only used to handling horses. He, therefore, 'recommended that a thoroughly competent driver for the Motor Fire Engines be appointed on delivery of the first Engines and would also be a member of the Police Force'.

The post was advertised and in December 1913 there were a number of applicants for the position.

On 5 February 1914 orders for a Motor Fire Engine were placed by the Watch Contact No.1 with Dennis Brothers (1913) and Watch Contact No.2 with Leyland Motors and they were to be insured with the Royal Insurance Company at £22 a year for each Engine. The story goes that the first vehicle to arrive was the Dennis Motor Fire Engine. The Police wanted the Engineer, who had delivered it, to join the Police and become driver for the Brigade but he declined the offer as he was not interested.

The men had had no experience with a Motor Fire Engine, having been used to the Steamer and the older type of Engine and were not familiar a motor pump nor a motorised vehicle. However, the new Dennis-Tamini Motor Pump was placed in the Engine House and the Leyland-Mather & Platt Pump arrived a little later. It was delivered by William Nicholson from Leyland in Lancashire where he was a qualified engineer. While he was there he was asked to take a look at the Dennis. He checked over the Engine and made minor adjustments. Before he left, he was offered the job as

Open Day at Central Fire Station, Manor Road 1915. Superintendent GW Byne poses with his staff and their Leyland-Mather & Platt Motor Pump No. 2. Seated behind the steering wheel is William Nicholson

Mr William H Nicholson who became Chief Fire Officer

Engineer which he accepted. However, he was also offered the job as the driver of the Motor Fire Engines and Inspector of the Fire Brigade at a salary of £2.10s.0d a week in January 1913.

Mr. Nicholson was provided with a special Chief's hat which cost the Police eleven shillings. Mr Nicholson had married at the age of 26 and had a son and daughter. The family found digs in Queen Street. This house and No.4 were owned by Messrs. Thomas A Edwards and Co. and were rented on a ten year lease to the Fire Brigade for eight shillings a week plus rates. They were cleaned and painted by WH Roberts for a cost of £12.15s.0d.

Mr Nicholson, like the other firemen, would place the legs of his trousers into his boots at night, so as to dress more quickly when there was a call-out.

PC. AJ Barnaby became Assistant Motor Engineer.

The Brigade now had two similar Motor Pumps, the other being the Dennis-Tamini Pump Escape.

The Watch Committee wanted to inspect the new Leyland Engine that had arrived at the Fire Station so Mr. Nicholson took the Engine, registration No. HF93, down to the Town Hall and a number of members of the Committee were taken out for a ride on the Appliance. Holding onto the brass rail and looking very important they set off. They were driven around Seacombe but no one had told Mr Nicholson that the main road was at the top of Oakdale Road and he drove into Wheatland Lane without stopping and collided with a tramcar, knocking it off the lines!

Mr Nicholson boasted how wonderful Leyland Engines were, being able to derail a tramcar.

Some years later there was an accident involving one of the Appliances, Mr Nicholson laid down the law saying that the driver could not have been looking what he was doing.

Walter Meacock quietly reminded him, "How long ago was it, sir, that you knocked the tram off the lines?"

"On your way", was the reply.

Leyland started business on steam engines and later produced steam-powered lawn mowers.

Being approached by the Chief Fire Officer in Dublin in 1909 with his own plans they built their first fire engine and others followed. The Mather and Platt turbine pump was able to deliver 250 gallons per minute. The fire engine was capable of reaching 60mph. An 85 BHP six-cylinder engine was added to the range in the latter part of 1910.

The break-blocks operated on the drive-shaft which were applied by means of the break-lever in the controls of the Breakman. The Engine carried a 60ft. Wheeled Escape which weighed about 2,000lbs. and had special mountings. The men would jump up onto the Engine to release it and bring it to the ground so that it could be wheeled off to where it was needed. The men grabbed the handles and wound up the ladder to the desired height. Escapes were very well balanced which made them easy to handle.

The old Escape-Pump Engine had solid rubber tyres. The polished brass bell was mounted by the passenger seat next to the driver and was used to warn other road-users that they were hurrying to a fire and to let those at the fire know that help was on the way.

Brass oil-lamps were clipped either side of the cab and two large headlamps were placed either side of the radiator with a bugle-type horn fixed face downwards with the rubber bulb next to the driver's seat. There was ample room for the Firemen on either side of the Engine.

An Engine going to a fire would have one officer, a driver and three or four men, one acting as Breakman.

The hard solid rubber tyres of the first two Motor Engines were later replaced with pneumatic ones with a windscreen added and also other modifications. Engine Drivers and Boiler Firemen were granted 8-9 hours shift.

In 1914 Fireman Bob Herron was living at No.12 and Fireman Robert Johnson at No.30. Soon after, Ernest Platt, the Brigade engineer, lived next door to the Fire Station at 4 Manor Road.

By 1917, Ernest Lindsay Paton, Engineer, lived at No.4, Bob Heron was at No.12 and at No.34 was PC Joe Atkinson, who became a Fire Bobby. Police Sergeant William Davies, lived here in 1925. It could be that No.4 and No.6 were looked upon as part of the Fire Station No.2 being the Station itself. Mr Nicholson was responsible to the Chief Constable for the discipline and efficiency of his Department; the maintenance of the Fire Pumps and Appliances; the Ambulances that were attached to his Department as well as any police vehicles. He was also responsible for the records relating to the testing of the hydrants in the town.

******

Fire Bobbies

A better man by a half-of-crown
By a half-a-crown?
By a half-a-crown.
Yes, two-and-six is half-a-crown.

WS Gilbert

The Fire Brigade was now under the care of the Wallasey Borough Council but soon after the town became a County Borough, the Council decided that the Fire Brigade should become the responsibility of the Police. Therefore, in 1914 the Fire Service came under Police supervision and its personnel became Police Officers. The Chief Constable became Director of the Wallasey Police Fire Brigade which meant it was under his control. In his report he said:

"*The permanent staff of the Fire Brigade is nine, one whom is a member of the Police Force. Four Constables are also members of the Brigade and receive an allowance in addition to their pay. It is intended to increase the number and for the present the remainder of the Police Force are to act as Firemen when required and paid for attending at fires according to scale.*"

For the first hour, they received a half a crown and each additional hour they got a shilling.

The Firemen were on the same level as the Police Constables and received the same basic pay. The Fire Bobbies went on to receive ten shillings a Call-Out and the Station Log Book was filled in by the Dutyman.

An old log book existed for many years at the fire station. Such entries concerned the horses eg. "Billy unwell". This horse died and another was hired until a replacement was found.

The Motor Engineer received the same rate as 16th year rate for Constables. The Fireman's pay in 1918 was:-

6th year 36 shillings a week
7th year 37 shillings a week
8th year 38 shillings a week
10th year 39 shillings a week
12th year 40 shillings a week.

Mr. Barry, the Chief Constable, always had the intention to dispense with the services of the Auxiliary Firemen as several members of the Force had had Fire Brigade experience and these men could take their place and would receive two shillings and six pence a week acting as Firemen and one shilling and three pence for each succeeding hour. For attendance at Fire Drill in overtime they received one shilling and six pence per drill.

For duty, duty must be done;
The rule applies to every one,
And painful though that duty be,
To shirk the task were fiddle-de-dee!

WS Gilbert

Eventually there were 14 Fire Bobbies to man the Brigade and Ambulance Service. All Fire Bobbies wore the letters 'FB' on their tunics, carried a Warrant Card and in theory had the power to arrest any person breaking the law. Their prime duty was to the Fire Brigade and after a period they would return to police duties and could be called upon when required.

The Inspectors' uniform for the Fire Brigade was of reefer serge and the Superintendent's was made by Mr. Hugh Frame of Liverpool. Other uniforms were supplied by Messrs. Reynolds and Co. Firemen's caps cost three shilling and six pence each.

Fireman T Highton had his pay increased to 34 shillings a week and Fireman Herbert Winstanley's wage went up to thirty shillings in April 1932 for long service.

Many of the Fire Brigades were supplied with Hudson whistles which were carried by the Firemen and could be useful in contacting each other whilst attending a fire.

Police Constables carried their number on the collar of their tunics so the public could report them in an event of complaint. When the Firemen became separate (from the Police) the Authorities wanted the men also to have numbers on their tunics but they decided against it. However, all the Firemen were allocated a number in order to know who was exactly on the pump whilst fighting a fire.

The Birkenhead Brigade became a Municipal Brigade but Liverpool remained under the direction of the Police which had been founded in 1837 with help of the insurance companies who also had their own Firemen and contributed towards its upkeep until 1941. The Liverpool Brigade wore silver helmets.

In July 1914 Fire Call Boxes were set up in Brighton Street and Bell Road by the Post Office for which the Brigade was charged an annual rental of £11.12s.6d.

In 1914 there had been two False Alarms and the Council taking a dim view of the matter, decided to offer 10 shillings reward to anyone giving information leading to the conviction of any person giving a False Alarm.

Two more Auxiliary Firemen joined on 13 August 1914.

Ambulance Service

The Seacombe Station was later used as an Ambulance Station. Tenders were sought for a new Motor Ambulance in April 1914 and an order was placed with the West Coast Motor Company to supply a 40 horse power Daimler Motor Ambulance in May 1914 at a cost of £682. It was insured for £14 per annum. It had doors for the driver and attendant on either side of the cab but did not have glass in the upper portion. The vehicles were painted dark green and had small side windows but none at the rear. The single door at the rear had a brass handle with rather a crude stretcher inside. These Ambulances were withdrawn 1949/50. One was left in the Fire Station yard and the local children used play in it. New Daimlers were to take their place at a later date. When the police took over the Fire Service in Wallasey, they had at least two motor Ambulances which were kept at the Central Fire Station.

In 1915, the Prison Commissioners paid £20 annually for conveying prisoners to Walton Gaol.

Tenders were sort for a Petrol Motor Wagon with interchangeable water tank and two trailers.

The Central Fire Station was officially opened in Manor Road on 23 October 1915. The Mayor of Wallasey, Benjamin Swanwick, is seen with Town Councillors, including Alderman Sidney Dawson, Alderman Edwin Peace, Alderman Thomas Burrows, Alderman Francis Storey and others

Children are seen admiring the Fire Engines at the Central Fire Station in Manor Road, Liscard.
The Dennis-Tamini Pump is in No.2 bay and the Leyland-Mather & Platt Pump in No.3 bay

New Fire Station

The Borough Surveyor costed the erection of a new Fire Station at £5,500 and the purchase of the Superintendent Byne's house next door for £360. Permission was granted in 1914 for the new Central Fire Station to be built and work started on the new building in Manor Road, replacing the old converted barn-type and Public Weighing Machine buildings. While it was being built, a temporary pole was erected in the entry to carry the telephone wires that were connected to the Firemen's homes. The new building of red-pressed brick and sandstone had four bays, each bay had a folding door with glass at the top portion. Above were the words 'Wallasey Central Fire Station' (one word to each bay) and an office (Control Room) at the side of the building with a door that opened on to the pavement. A large map of the Borough was on the wall of the room so that the driver could see at a glance where the fire was. A fine stone Wallasey Coat of Arms was placed under the apex above the Control Room.

I can remember my father lifting me up to see through the windows of the folding doors to enable me to see the smartly polished Fire Engines. Similar doors were at the reverse end to enable the Engines to be backed into the good-sized Parade Yard at the rear of the building.

The rooms above consisted of a recreation room with two smooth, solid metal poles that went down through a hole to the ground floor, enabling the Firemen to slide down and get to the Appliances within seconds; a Mess Room; Billiards Room; Kitchen and two toilets. There were also two baths which the Firemen could use after attending a fire. The seating, cupboards and fixtures cost £71.13s.0d. The other furniture and bedding supplied by GW Jervis amounting to £45.18s.6d.

The prime purpose of the tower, which was 58ft. high was to dry the 100 ft. hose. If water was left in the old rubber-lined hose without being drained, it turned into acid and could burn the Firemen or his clothes.

The building was designed by Mr TW Travers, the Borough

Engineer and built by the well-known family firm headed by Mr James A Milestone who lived in Manor Mansions in Manor Road. Other local buildings erected by them included:- St Columbia's, at the junction of Seabank Road and Trafalgar Avenue, Egremont; St Thomas', Seaview Road; the *Black Horse Inn; Traveller's Rest* and Vernon's Flour Mill, Seacombe (1898). The new Fire Station cost £5,517 and was officially opened on Saturday 23 October 1915 when local dignities assembled for the occasion. The Mayor of Wallasey, Benjamin Swanwick and Town Councillors were present. Six wooden tubs with evergreens were placed outside the Fire Station.

The *Wallasey News* had this to say:-

The new Fire Station has at last been completed and is now in use. It should give the greatest satisfaction to Wallaseyans, as for many years the borough has had an efficient fire brigade under the command of Superintendent Byne, but not for an efficient fire station; perhaps it would be better to say a convenient fire station, for the old barn with its long and chequered history which in recent years had housed the Engines had been made as efficient as possible, and it is remarkable under the circumstances that the brigade should have maintained the high standard that it has done in the past.

Whilst the Fire Station was being built, the Wallasey Taxi-Cab Company offered the use of their premises that were behind the Fire Station for a rental of £50 for twelve months. The Council agreed to the offer.

I cleaned the windows and I swept the floor,
And I polished up the handle of the big front door.
WS Gilbert

The usual practice after morning parade saw the men take up their positions on the appliances. The Duty Office would give the order for the bells to be tested, the Engines switched on and the men climbed aboard. If the Duty Officer was satisfied, the next job was cleaning the brass including the bells, radiators and headlamps.

Wallasey Firemen, with collecting nets for charity, are waiting to join a Parade in 1918 with Herbert Winstanley on the Motor Pump and PC Jim Gallagher standing by

All the equipment had to be checked, the floors scrubbed and windows cleaned. The hoses had to be inspected and in some cases washed and scrubbed then hung up in the tower to dry.

In 1915, the Brigade dealt with 46 alarms and the Ambulance was called out 176 times.

With the Dennis-Tamini Pump-Escape No.1 and the Leyland-Mather & Platt Motor Pump No.2, Wallasey had an efficient Brigade.

When there was a Call-Out (or a 'Shout' as some Firemen like to say), the Firemen would slide down the pole and scramble onto the Engine. One man would operate the folding doors and another would stand in the middle of the road and hold up the traffic. The Appliances would then be on their way to the scene of the fire within minutes of receiving the call.

******

Sprites of earth and air
Friends of flame and fire.

WS Gilbert

The Palace Fire

The old Palace amusement building on the promenade at New Brighton caught fire in April 1916 which destroyed the greater part of the complex but the Brigade was able to save the old Gaiety Theatre and Skating Rink. The theatre, which had been opened in about 1890 with the name of The Palace and Pavilion Theatre, became a cinema in 1903 and was the first hall in the town to show animated pictures. The owners wanted to demolish it and rebuild. However it was not to be and the Council purchased the land for £41,500 under the Wallasey Tramways and Improvement Act of 1907. However, it continued as a cinema and theatre until 1926 and was demolished in 1933.

Wounded Soldiers

The newly built Town Hall in Brighton Street (Foundation Stone was laid by King George V on 25 March 1914) was opened as a Military Hospital on 12 August 1916 as an auxiliary to the Military Hospital in Fazakerley. It was not long before the first wounded men arrived. Over 300 beds were in various parts of the building and the medical staff treated over 3,500 patients from 1916 to 1919. It was not opened as municipal offices until 3 November 1920 the year Wallasey became a Parliamentary Borough.

Wounded soldiers were also cared for at the Cenacle Red Cross Hospital at the top of Atherton Street in New Brighton. This old house was called "Sandrock" and had been purchased in 1912 by the French Roman Catholic Order for the Sisters the Cenacle as a nunnery. The Red Cross treated some 700 soldiers here.

The foundation stone for the Liverpool Open-air Hospital was laid by Lord Derby and the first portion of the building was opened 21 July 1914.

Superintendent Byne took ill in January 1918 and his assistant, Mr Nicholson, took charge of the brigade in his absence. During My Byne's illness, the chemist's account amounted to £3.11.5d which was paid by the Council.

Sadly Mr Byne did not recover from his illness. William Nicholson received an extra 15 shillings a week pay, back-dated from 1 May 1918 and on 11 July 1918 he was appointed Officer in Charge of the Wallasey Fire Brigade with a salary of £180 per annum, increasing to £200 with the rank and grade of Inspector. He was responsible to the Chief Constable for discipline and the general efficiency of his department. He was responsible for maintenance of the fire pumps and appliances as well as the ambulance that was attached to the department together with any vehicles that were attached to the Police department. He was also responsible for the records relating to the testing of the hydrants in the town. Mr Nicholson's salary was increased from £200 to £210 but the two shillings rent allowance was abolished.

The Chief Constable engaged Isaac Cowan as Auxiliary Motor Mechanic for the Brigade on 15 May 1918, with pay of 53 shillings a week. William Ormsby Pooley, who had been discharged from the army, was employed by the Wallasey Fire Brigade as a motor driver from 18 May 1918.

A Motor Ambulance was purchased from the Quality Coal Company Ltd. at a cost of £210 in June 1918 for the use at Mill Lane Hospital. The Austin Ambulance was repaired at the cost of £33.

The Chief Constable recommended that Arthur William Say became a Constable and Driver for the Fire Brigade in July 1918. Also in that year, the price of 100ft. lengths of two & threequarter inch hose was £92.15s and couplings cost 25 shillings each.

Dock Explosion

Tragedy struck on 25 September 1918 at about 11am when there was an explosion in the West Float resulting in death of five men and eight seriously injured. The explosion shook the whole district and people hurried down to the docks. The accident happened on board an oil vessel belonging to the Anglo-American Oil Company, which was lying on the Poulton side of the West Float Dock, while a number of men were repairing one of the deck petroleum tanks. Coal gas had mixed with fumes from the benzine and petrol causing the explosion. Fire Brigades from both Wallasey and Birkenhead attended. Fireman Driscoll from the Wallasey Brigade quickly got together the trained ambulance men from Government stores to help with the injured. The Lady Superintendent and a nurse at the depot all administered first aid.

A girl operator on the switchboard from Uveco Mills, who had telephoned the Brigade, did gallant work in sending messages throughout the day.

The ship on which the explosion had occurred was on the far side of another vessel that was moored against the quayside. The explosion had ripped a portion of the deck and hatchway and blown onto the steamer lying alongside, causing the bridge and upper deck to catch fire.

The side of the vessel near the stern was also blown out. Dense volumes of smoke rose from the ship and suffocating fumes made it difficult for the Firemen to work.

The local newspaper said . . . *and their bravery with which they accomplished their task under such difficult conditions is beyond praise.*

Three lengths of hose were used by the Wallasey Fire Brigade, pumping water from the dock and in a short time the fire was brought under control.

The Firemen working on the coal bunkers were brought up by one of the ship's Officers including: Second Officer Beasley of Birkenhead Fire Brigade; Inspector Nicholson, Firemen Dolan and Fradley and Acting Sergeant Atkinson of Wallasey Fire Brigade who had descended into the hold despite the suffocating fumes. The seamen who had been injured or overcome with poisonous gases were brought up by the aid of ropes and lowered derricks. William Joy, aged 26, from Higher Tranmere was one of the men killed at the scene. Edward Williams of Rock Ferry and James Harris of Birkenhead, died later as result of their injuries

The injured were taken to the Victoria Central Hospital and Birkenhead Borough Hospital by Ambulance, which included the Wallasey Freemasons' Ambulance – presented to the Corporation in March 1918.

Edward Garland of 6 Brook Place Wallasey, Samuel Forsyth of Liscard, B Fairless (South Shields), Daniel Offlangs (Bootle), Patrick Wilson (Liverpool), G Toddy (West Kirby), W Wright (Birkenhead), Patrick Sweeney (Liverpool), William Nugent (Birkenhead) and a Japanese gentleman were all badly injured. The Chief Engineer, Bert Gidney of Bootle was reported to be missing. Both Mr Forsyth and Mr Fairless, died the following day. The Mayor of Birkenhead, Alderman M Byrne, opened a fund for the relief of the dependents.

******

1919

In 1919, the Wallasey Fire Brigade staff consisted of one Inspector, one Sergeant and 11 Police Fire Constables when they had 50 Call Outs, three which proved to be False Alarms. It was estimated that £18,000 damage had been done to property due to fires.

The Brigade complained of the poor water supply in the town.

The cost of maintaining the Brigade for year ending 31 March 1919 was £2,257 compared with £1,610 for the previous year.

Six 100ft. lengths of two and threequarter inch hose was purchased from Messrs. McGregor of Dundee at the cost of £93.15s.

Mr and Mrs Nicholson and their family, consisting of Mary and Richard Hornby, went to live in the Superintendent's house in Anglesey Road. Richard went on to study Law and became Prosecuting Officer for Liverpool. Mrs Byne, the former Superintendent's widow, had vacated the house and the Council gave her £10 towards the removal.

More Fires

A fire broke out on Monday 15 March 1920 at the Liver Chain Works of Messrs. J Parr Ltd. on the corner of Addington Road and Hartismere Road, Poulton. At four o'clock, flames were seen shooting out of the skylight and soon the roof fell in. The Fire Brigade were summoned and although the flames had a hold on the building, the Firemen prevented the flames from spreading to the nearby buildings and after two hours was under control.

A few days later, Constable Carroll was on foot patrol in New Brighton at 4am when he spotted smoke coming from the Tivoli Theatre. He summoned the Fire Station and woke the theatre attendant. When the Firemen arrived, the theatre was filled with smoke. However, under the direction of Inspector Nicholson the flames were tackled – fortunately a new water main had recently been installed outside which helped to extinguish the flames and the auditorium was saved from serious damage. However, the estimated cost of the damage caused by the water and fire, which had been started by a cigarette, amounted to £1,000.

The Isle of Man Ferry King Orry *stranded at New Brighton on 21 August 1921. Firemen are seen on long ladders rescuing those that wanted to leave the ship*

Aground!

The Wallasey Fire Brigade answered an unusual Call-Out on 19 August 1921 when the Isle of Man Steam Packet *King Orry* ran aground on New Brighton beach near Perch Rock Lighthouse. She had left Douglas at nine o'clock that morning and was met with dense fog on entering the Mersey. As the tide went out passengers on the stranded vessel looked down at the sandbank below. The Wallasey Fire Brigade was summoned and the Firemen used the Escape and ladders to get many passengers off the boat but some decided to stay on. The ship was towed off by tugs at high water and returned to service a few days later

The Bell System

The Bell System, which connected the station to the homes of Firemen as far away as Wimbledon Street, was installed by Herbert Winstanley and operated successfully for a number of years. The Fire Bell was fixed on a bedroom wall and a series of rings summoned them:

One Ring - A Fireman was wanted at the Fire Station.

Two Rings - 'A Private Case'. A man was needed for Ambulance Duty when a patient would have to be collected and taken to hospital.

Three Rings - An accident had occurred. The men would have to run to the Fire Station.

Four Rings - indicated that the Chief Fire Officer wanted a Fireman.

One Long Ring - of 45 seconds meant that there was a fire.

The system was pendulum operated making it alternate for a full minute.

Today, country part-timers, are given a bleeper to summon them to the Fire Station.

A Wheeled Escape was kept outside the Fire Station that could be used to mend the wires when they got broken. The men received extra pay for attending to the wires.

Other Wheeled Escapes were left in various parts of the Borough as the Brigade did not always have the vehicles to transport them.

On the Ready

'Gunner' Marshall like other Firemen, would have his clothes at the ready. His trousers were worn over his heavy leather jack boots to get dressed quicker.

When there was a fire, men would be seen running down Manor Road wearing jack boots and pulling their shirts on. The rest of the clothing could be put on while they were on the Fire Engine. They would have to hold onto the rail with one hand to make sure they were not thrown off the vehicle as it swung around the corners and try to get their jackets on and buttoned up with the other.

Left to Right: Gunner Marshall, Plum Warner,
Herbert Winstanley and Sgt. Joseph Holt

The bell that was hung in the turret of the older Fire Station to call the Firemen, when it was no longer needed, was given to Central Park as a closing-bell.

The Police-Firemen now were living in 'Tied Houses' in Manor Road and Barnwell Avenue.

It was considered using the new building as a temporary hospital during the First War World but it was not suitable.

All calls for the Fire Brigade came through the Police Station using the telephone No. Liscard 47 and then directed to the Fire Station requested. Seacombe Fire Station was No. 44 and Wallasey Village No. 229

Eventually, there were 14 Police Firemen to man the Fire Brigade and Ambulance whose minimum height was five feet, eight and a half inches.

The old cottages by the Fire Station in Manor Road, known as the Firemen's Cottages, were probably built in 1884 for the soldiers of the Cheshire Regiment, known as the 'Greys' on account of their uniform, who had their Drill Hall in Urmson Road (a large garage was later built on the site). The cottages were built of local sandstone with pretty little front gardens. They originally had a kitchen, living room, two bedrooms, no bathroom and an outside toilet. The floors were stone flagged. They were occupied by the Firemen who had to be near the Fire Station as in those days they had to live within hearing of the Station's Fire Bell. The cottages are now Grade 2 Listed buildings.

The next row of houses were known as *Hughes Cottages*, followed by *Manor Terrace* with *Park View* and *Northcote Villas* on the opposite side of the road.

Changing Scene

Liscard Village had changed over the years. Opposite the old Fire Station was Urmson's (or Urmston's) House which had been built sandstone in 1729 being a good example of the second seventeenth century period of building. It was at, one time, known as Liscard Hall (before the hall in Central Park was built). Mr. J Urmson lived there who was a yeoman farmer and had land near Townfield Lane. This lane was later called Urmson Road, after him. The building was ivy-covered and had railings in front. It had a slated roof, was three storeys high and two doors opened onto the pavement. Next door was a slated barn-type building with high doors. These buildings were demolished in 1928.

The tall three storey stone cottages (Townfield Buildings) that stood at the bottom of Urmson Road were built as homes for the quarrymen. The White Delph Quarry between Withens Lane and Rake Lane was owned by Mrs Maddock, the Lady of the Manor. The old 'Monkey House' pagoda-type public shelter with wooden seats that had stood in the middle of the cross roads since 1904 was demolished in 1926 with gentlemen's toilets remaining underneath.

Hebron Hall had been built on the site of Egerton Cottage and Egerton Grove School had been built in 1928. Mr Higgins was Head Master. A large cinema was built on the site of Gibbons' Stables. At the age of 21 in 1921, Harry Ellison and his brother had opened a paint and wallpaper shop.

Stephen Gibbons had a fine garage and yard built for his funeral motors-cars and William Gibbons lived in a house called Inglefield by the front gates. The shops were set back and among these were Miss Strong's ladies hairdressing business, Mr Addyman, the leather merchant, Mr Dodd, the optician. Walter Crossland had a small printing business and later moved to a house in Manor Road.

Prospect Place and Prospect Cottages were still standing.

Liscard Village was now the centre of the town; traffic had increased.

The old Liscard Hall Farm had been demolished and Trafford House built on the site, remaining until 1913 when the General Post Office was built on the part of the ground.

The old *Queen's Arms Hotel* was on the corner of Queens Street and there was a stable next door. Above was a room where the Wallasey Commissioners first held their meetings. This stable was still being used in the late 1930s.

******

The Winstanley Family

I am so proud,
If I allowed
My family pride
To be my guide.

WS Gilbert

One of the earliest members of the Wallasey Fire Brigade was Herbert Winstanley who was a volunteer Fireman living in Wallasey Village. He died in the First World War while serving in the Army. He had been posted to the Isle of Man and was guarding prisoners over there when he caught typhoid. He had a Military Funeral in Wallasey and when the hearse passed the Fire Station, all the Engines were brought out and the bells put down. The family were living in Wallasey Village at the time.

His son, Herbert, was named after him and he in turn had four sons, Herbert, Jack, Leslie and Arthur, who all except Arthur joined the Fire Service.

Herbert (II) joined the Police as PC No.76, in November 1911 who was later drafted into the Fire Brigade becoming a permanent Fire Bobby and was later promoted to the rank of Sergeant. He married and lived at 1 Prospect Cottages in Liscard Village being a joiner by trade. They had three daughters and four sons. His son, Herbert, was born on the day of the New Brighton Tower fire in 1915.

In those days Firemen wore polished brass helmets and Herbert II's was passed down to son Les and at the present time is in Germany.

It was expected of him to be able to reach the Fire Station in 45 seconds in daytime and one and a half minutes at night.

The family then moved to 4 Manor Road which was part of the Fire Station where twins Jack and Les were born. They later moved to No. 29 on the other side of the road. He became driver to Mr Nicholson in the Chief's Armstrong-Siddley automatic. He suffered a leg injury while pushing one of the Fire Engines. The youngest of the children, Pamela married and went to live in the Isle of Man. She now writes and illustrates little books about a cat called Manxie.

When there was a fire at the mills, Mrs. Winstanley would go

22

Herbert Winstanley II

down and take a jug of hot cocoa for the Firemen and her children went along to watch the fire. Young Jack was a two-year-old and little did his mother think that her boys would follow their father and join the Fire Service when they grew up. Her son, 11 year-old Herbert, had been invited to the Mayor's Party at the Town Hall. She had bought him a new suit of clothes and a pair shoes for the occasion. This was quite an effort on a Fireman's pay. Young Herbert would have sooner gone to the watch the fire than attend the function but all he saw of it was the flames as he looked out of the window.

A moderate livelihood we`re gaining.
In fact we rule
A National School.
The duties are dull, but I'm not complaining.
This sort of thing takes a deal of training!
WS Gilbert

The boys attended St Mary's Church School, Liscard Road, then Central School, Vaughan Road School, New Brighton. They would, like many other boys at that time, go around and collect horse manure and sell it to people for their gardens at two pence a bucket in order to save up to go to the Isle of Man. There was plenty of money to be made when the circus came to Wallasey and they followed the elephants from Brick Field (now the site of the telephone Exchange) to Delph field in Rake Lane.

Herbert Winstanley (II) was stationed at the Seacombe Fire Station in Brougham Road for a time. He designed a vehicle for the Brigade that would lay the hose. Herbert (III), while working on the airfield at Hooton, explained the workings of this hose-laying machine and was asked to make them one.

If an aircraft was coming in with undercarriage difficulty an RAF Foam Vehicle would go out with a man standing by with an asbestos suit ready to wear. The Firemen would follow up with Herbert's vehicle and lay the hose and when the Foam Unit had finished their task, the Firemen would spray the aircraft with water.

The Fire Chief, Mr Washburn, decided to go one better. He put the Stand-Pipe down and connected the hose to it so as the Firemen ran out with the machine the water was almost ready to use. This idea, however, was not always successful.

In his younger days, Herbert (III) would go cycling into Wales with his future wife on a tandem and later with a motorcycle. They have a son who was also named Herbert and for a time was a Firemen at Port Sunlight.

Herbert (II) was also interested in building and repairing wireless sets and could also repair old wind-up gramophones. He had one taken to pieces and asked his friend to hold the powerful spring very tightly. Just then the fire bells went down and Herbert had to rush out with the Fire Engine. He was away for about an hour and when he lot back the friend was still holding it! His wife had bound a scarf around his hands and could not let go if he wanted to.

The Firemen were on duty at the Central Station on an eight hours shift, they would spend their time playing snooker whilst on call. Herbert was an excellent player but did not gamble, smoke or drink alcohol.

Herbert (II) was kept on after the Second World War and when he did retire from the Fire service he returned to his trade as a general contractor and was well known for driving to work in his motorcycle with his Spaniel, Rover, travelling in the side car. Another of their dogs was a black spaniel in the 1940s called Dusky who stole a string of sausages from Bell's the butcher and raced up the road with them hanging from his jaws!.

Arthur Winstanley was stationed abroad in the Army for three years during in the Second World War and on his return home on leave, he stepped off the bus outside Whitby's Dairy in Manor Road and found his dog there to meet him. He later learned that the animal had been on edge all day.

He was a regular soldier with the King's Liverpool Regiment and was posted to Prestatyn and given ten rounds of ammunition and rifle and a bicycle and had to patrol the whole area and keep a lookout for the enemy!

Parachutist

Arthur fought in North Africa and Italy then was parachuted into Arnhem in 1944 and fought in the battle. He was injured, taken prisoner, attempted to escape three times and finally being successful was at large for six weeks until he found the American Forces then returned home. He was Guest of Honour at the VE Day Celebrations in Wallasey Village.

In 1999, at the age of 77, he intended to make the 15,000ft. parachute jump to celebrate the 55th Anniversary of the Battle of Arnhem, but due to a fall on a train, was unable to do so. However, he was successful in 2001 making a tandem jump.

Manor Road Cottages where many Firemen and their
families lived, including the Winstanley family

Firemen of the Birkenhead Fire Brigade are assembled outside the home of James Williams in Tansley Terrace, Newton; a colleague who died on 16 November 1921 (See this page)

On one occasion Herbert (II) was called out to a fire but was not sure where it was as the caller failed to say. However, he followed the crowd who were running along the street to see the fire!

When there was a three-bell alarm for a grass fire at Harrison Park, Herbert and his sons would all set off and using beaters or their coats would put out the burning grass.

Herbert Winstanley was in charge of checking Fire hydrants around the borough to see that they were in good working order. He would go around on foot taking either Arthur or Herbert with him. There was even one in a back garden that few people knew existed. He would connect up to a stand-pipe and get it to run for a while. Often a lady would ask him to wash her drive. Mr Winstanley would oblige.

Sometimes a cat would get stuck up in a tree and they would send for the Fire Brigade. They would not use the machine so Herbert would take the Escape ladder and young Herbert would go along with him. When the cat was rescued, the owner wanted to give him a tip.

"We are not allowed to accept tips, madam", said Herbert, "but you can give the lad something if you like."

Another task for Herbert was to call on all the theatres and cinemas in the town to see that they met with fire regulations.

Jack Winstanley married and went to live in one of the small cottages in Wallasey Village when he joined the Wallasey Fire Service. He then joined Cheshire County Fire Brigade followed by a move to London and became Senior Instructor at Moreton-in-Marsh before returning to Wallasey as Station Officer. He also served in London where he was connected with breathing apparatus. He was offered a job in Oldham as Assistant Divisional Officer but turned it down and was once in charge at Ellesmere Port. During the Second World War he was a parachutist in the army.

When he was Station Officer at Wallasey he was always 'Jack' to his old friends in the Brigade, but the younger men called him 'Sir'. All men addressed him as 'Sir' when on a fire.

In those days, Station Officers used to have three days on and one day off. Nowadays, they are like Watch Officers.

Jack Winstanley and his wife now live in Newton and he still has the white helmet, old hose and nozzle in the loft that was once used in the children's hospital in Leasowe.

Leslie Winstanley was a Leading Fireman at Wallasey then went to Connah's Quay Fire Brigade and finally to Oxford Fire Brigade.

Herbert (III) was a joiner by trade and served in the Fire Service during the blitz in Second World War along with brother-in-law Tom Nichols and Len Barnes. He had put his application in for Full-Time membership of the Wallasey Fire Brigade but Mr Nicholson was away so he had to go to see the Chief Constable, John Ormerod to put his application in but was not successful.

After the war he returned to his trade where he had a workshop in Selby Street for 35 years. Married for over 60 years with five grandchildren and two great grandchildren, he lived in one of the cottages in Manor Road and keeps his old leather Jack boots as a memento.

The Winstanley family have been members of the Fire Service for many years and one could have called it 'Winstanley's Fire Brigade'. Indeed, there was one occasion when there was a Call-Out to a fire in Albion Street, New Brighton, with Herbert (II) in charge; sons Herbert (III) and Jack and twin brother, Les; and son-in-law, Tom Garner as driver!

Leslie later went to live down South and became a Station Officer. He died in 1997.

Jack's uncle was Divisional Chief Officer in Cambridge in the days before the Second World War; his son was Station Officer with Birkenhead Fire Brigade, recently retiring; a nephew is a member of the Prestatyn Fire Brigade and another nephew, Brian Parry, became a Fireman with Wallasey Fire Brigade retiring as its longest serving member in 1998 and took part in the Winston Churchill Travelling Fellowship which him took him across America. He holds the Winston Churchill Memorial Medal which was presented to him by Sir Winston's grandson..

The family have received four good conduct Silver Medals. Grandfather Herbert for 20 years' service; his son, also Herbert, for 35 years' service; Jack for 25 years' service and his son also has a medal.

The Winstanley family must be one of the oldest Fire Brigade families in England and I feel proud to have met them and to have been welcomed in their homes. They are truly a remarkable family.

******

The 1920s

In the early 1920s there were about 3,400 full-time Firemen in the country; London Fire Brigade having some 1,300 Officers and men to operate their 65 Fire Stations and three River Stations.

All the London Firemen then lived at the Station with single men in dormitories (for which they paid a shilling a week) and married men with children had small two-roomed flats being charged various rates according to the length of service.

Accident

A tragic accident happened on Armistice Day 11 November 1921 at Hamilton Square, Birkenhead when a maroon exploded causing serious injury to Fireman James Williams of the Birkenhead Fire

Brigade. He died five days later. The coffin was carried on one of many fire engines which led the procession from his home in Newton to St John's Church, Frankby (*see photograph*).

Changes

The Firemen in all Fire Brigades after a fire had to clean the Engines and test all the equipment so that it would be ready for the next Call-Out. The practice is still the same today.

The 54 hour week came in and a short leave of two or three hours a week and seven days annual.

In 1925, Mr Nicholson resided at the Station and had two Sergeants in Thomas Wilkinson and Joseph Atkinson.

There were also Police Auxiliary Firemen.

An extensive fire broke out on board the CPR liner *Montlaurier* on 15 April 1925 while the ship was undergoing repairs in Cammell Laird's shipyard, Birkenhead. The whole of the interior of the fore part of the liner was destroyed. Six Brigades, including Wallasey, attended the blaze that raged for ten hours

Grandstand Fire

There was a fire at the Tower Athletic Ground in the 1920s when, after a Boy Scout event had taken place the wicker beech chairs that were stored under the grandstand caught fire and the Brigade was called. The stand was badly damaged and the local residents had to be temporarily evacuated due to the threat from sparks starting further fires.

There was a fire in King Street, Egremont, at Garland's photography shop. A nursemaid was left in charge of their seven-year-old boy who seemed to have played with matches and set fire to the house. The boy was lost in the fire.

******

Boys of the Old Brigade

Little Bob Herron, whose father was a slaughterman at Cox's Slaughter House, was one of the early Fireman. He lived 1 Prospect Cottages in Liscard Village and drove the Horse-Drawn Engines in 1912. He moved to 12 Manor Road and later lived at No.7. Bob became a driver for the Motor Engines.

Other Firemen around at that time were Herbert Johnson who lived 30 Manor Road, George Joughin at 6 and Henry Holder at 10.

Some of the Firemen who lived in Manor Road in the 1920s were:-

No.4 Sgt. Thomas Wilkinson, later occupied by Mr Marsden then Sergeant William Davies, No.34 Police Sgt. Joseph Atkinson, No.7 Con. Fireman Robert (Bob) Francis Herron, No.9 Fireman Henry Joseph Dolan, No.6 Con. Fireman Richard Bertram Johnson, No.12 Con. Fireman Leonard Marsden, No.14 Con. Fireman Richard Webster, No.18 Con. Fireman George Roberts, No.30 Con. Fireman Arthur Edward Fradley.

Also listed then was Fireman Patrick Casey 5 Lancaster Avenue.

A Pre-War list of Personnel included:-

Mr. William Nicholson, Chief Fire Officer; Sgt. Joseph Holt; Sgt. Byrne, Jack ('Gunner') Marshall; Thomas Wilkinson; Lennie Marsden; Jack Williams (Mounted); Bob Herron; Bob Jones; Len Maddocks; Harry Benfield; Harry Dolan; Harold Cash; John Thorley; Frank Fradley; Walter Peach; Tommy Highton; Herbert Winstanley; Bert Clague and Tim Riley.

Superintendent William Nicholson went to live at 8 Barnwell Avenue where his telephone number was Wallasey 3484.

Leonard Marsden lived at 12 Manor Road; Richard Webster at 1 who was a Fireman and George Roberts at 18 was a Fire Bobby. On the other side of the road was Police Fireman Robert Herron at 7 and around the corner, in Arnold Street, were two Firemen, John Price at and Edward Jones at 8.

John Marsh was another Fire Bobby who lived at 2 Prospect Place and Bert Winstanley resided at 1 Prospect Cottages. He too,

was a Police Fireman. These cottages in Liscard Village were a minute away from the Fire Station.

A well-known local nurse was Nurse McCamley who lived in Manor Road and was known as 'The Little Grey Nurse'. She was blind in one eye, wore a long dress with a white collar, grey cape and bonnet with white ties, and carried a black bag.

She had a plate outside her house and was called 'an Accouchever' (Midwife).

Firemen and Policemen who were living in Manor Road in 1936 were:-

No.3 PC Jack Williams; 5 Fireman Robert Herron; 9 Fireman Robert Jones; 23 PC Edward Fradley; 29 Police Fireman Herbert Winstanley; 35 Police Sergeant Joseph Holt; 4 Police Fireman John Marshall; 6 Police Fireman Leonard Marsden; 14 Fireman Richard Webster. Nurse Isobella McCamley lived at 18.

In Wimbledon Street:-No. 23 Police Fireman James Warner; 4 Police Fireman Harold Cash; 12 Police Constable George Robert Benfield.

In Egerton Grove:- No.12 Fireman Henry Dolan; 14 Police Constable Ivan Maddocks. Jonathan Thorley lived in Daventree Road.

Constable Benfield went to live at 38 Kenilworth Road, (probably related to Harry Benfield who lived in Wimbledon Street).

Jim Warner was always known as "Plum" Warner and was a regular member of the Fire Brigade.

Wally Leach, who was the youngest Fireman at the Station, married a nurse. Jack Marshall had served in the Royal Artillery during the First World War and was always known as 'Gunner Marshall'. He had three children and the family lived in Manor Road, moved to the other side of the road then to Barnwell Avenue. While on Police duty, he would foot patrol Harrison Drive.

Although I believe he got the name 'Gunner' through being in the Army, someone told me that he was known by that nickname because he often said that he was "gonna do this" or "gonna do that"!

At Christmas time he would dress up as Father Christmas for the Firemen's Annual Children's Party.

Harold Cash, who was known as 'Buddy' and later 'Ned', was quite young when he joined the Brigade having been a ship's Engineer. He had two sons, Jack and Neville. The latter worked at Cammell Laird. They lived in Egerton Grove before moving to Barnwell Avenue. Neville decided to go to sea and became an Officer. He married a local girl named Francis Whalley.

Harold Cash, who was well respected Fireman and had good Christian principles – being a nonsmoker and seldom drank alcohol – eventually became Deputy Chief Officer to Mr Nicholson.

When Harry Dolan retired from the Brigade, he took over as licensee of the *Royal Oak* public house in Liscard Village which was known as the 'Irish House', being popular with Irish labourers, who lived in nearby cottages working on local farms. An Irishman named Jimmy Creevey was licensee in 1916 who had played rugger in his younger days thus making it easy for him to throw out the unruly element when the occasion arose. It was a free house that sold no liquor and women were not allowed in.

Fireman Maddocks had been a Fire Bobby. He came from a religious family who named him Ivan Oswald Geoffrey Theodore which he hated and preferred to be called 'Bud'.

Tim Riley joined the Fire service just before the Second World War and was transferred to London, later returning to Wallasey to serve during the war years when he became Station Officer in charge of 'A' and 'B' Watches.

Mr. Walter Peach

Another popular member of the Wallasey Fire Brigade was Walter Peach (Wally to his colleagues), born 9 January 1916, he was one of the youngest members of the Brigade having started as a Fire Bobby. He retired from the Brigade in 1969 and he and his wife, Glyn, an ex-nurse, went to live in Llanasa in North Wales.

The Union Secretary wrote of him "a respected officer, and both a patient and practical man. But perhaps above all, the values we most miss will be that of a good comrade in whose company it was felt comforting to be in the heat of any job which the Brigade was committed." He pointed out how he had helped in the difficult times after the Second World War when the men returned to civilian life and took up new duties. He went on to say "It will be remembered that it was during those uncertain times, and often in the then somewhat alien atmosphere of the station, that the falterer would turn to Wally, 'the unruffled one', him who drew on his pipe for inspiration and shifted it three times before he spoke. Here was a shoulder to lean on and an ear to confide in. Walter was a steady friend and in respect of the common bond, became in '48 a foundation member of the Wallasey Branch and remained with us throughout."

Wally died on 1 March 1997.

Boys of the Fire Brigade

Where are the boys of the Fire Brigade,
Who fight with us side by side?
Shoulder to shoulder, hose and axe-blade,
Fought the flames 'til they've died!
Who so ready and undismayed?
Who were so merry and true?
They are the boys of the Fire Brigade.
Where are the lads we knew?

Then steadily shoulder to shoulder,
Steadily on the crusade!
Ready and strong, dashing along,
Are the boys of the Fire Brigade.

Pump Escape sets off in a mighty dash,
Driver Bob Herron at the steering-wheel.
" Ring the bell" orders Harold Cash
and 'Gunner' Marshall runs out the reel.
Up high go big clouds of black smoke.
Fireman Herbert Winstanley takes the hose,
"On with the water and give it a good soak!"
'Bud' turns it on and drenches his clothes!

Then steadily shoulder to shoulder,
Steadily on the crusade!
Ready and strong, dashing along,
Are the boys of the Fire Brigade!

Sergeant Holt and Fireman Wally Peach,
High up the ladder to the attic they climb.
The Sergeant is now able to reach,
That brave little fellow just in time!
Branches and escape are all stacked away,
The fire's now out, a job well done,
The Pump is now back in the bay.
And all reported to Mister Nicholson.

Then steadily shoulder to shoulder,
Steadily on the crusade!
Ready and strong, dashing along,
Are the boys of the Fire Brigade.

(With apologies to Fred E Weatherly)
******

Warehouse Fire

Paul's Grain Warehouse suffered a severe fire in 1924 on eight floors. The Firemen fought the flames for several hours and although it was some time before they got the fire under control, they managed to save the building.

The Gandy Fire

One of the worst fires in Wallasey before the Second World War was that of the Gandy Belt Company when on 18 February 1927 their factory in Seacombe caught fire. The fire alarm in the factory had sounded at about 3pm when there normally be about 300 men and women at the factory but they were on short-time. Most worked on the ground floor and it was soon cleared. Within a half an hour of the alarm, the fire made alarming progress on account of the strong northwest breeze. The fire had started in the middle of the building and soon the back wall collapsed. There was no space between the houses in Vernon Avenue and should the wind had been from the opposite direction nothing would have saved them. Twenty minutes after the Fire Brigade had been at the scene, there arose an acute shortage of water. When the supply was reintroduced, it proved to be inadequate. An earlier inspection showed that between 65 and 70 hydrants were duds.

The Brigade managed to prevent the fire from spreading to nearby houses. The middle wall crashed to the ground. The flames flew high into the black smoke. Inspector Nicholson was in charge of the Fire Brigade. Chief Constable Barry and Inspector Ormerod directed the Policemen. The Firemen were on duty for 24 hours - no knocking off at six o'clock in those days. The cause of the fire was understood to have been an electric light bulb that exploded above a tank containing oils and bitumen used for treating leather. The fire which could be seen from the Great Orme in North Wales, caused £250,000 worth of damage.

Loss of Fire Chief

Bootle Fire Brigade suffered the loss of their Chief Fire Officer Monk when he was killed following a fall while attending a fire at a cotton warehouse in Pacific Road in 1927. A large funeral was arranged with representatives of the crews from seven Brigades and the Liverpool Salvage Corps attending. The Wallasey Fire Brigade sent a Motor Pump and crew.

Tragedy

I am told that a little girl named Agnes Crombie who lived in Lancaster Avenue was burned to death in the 1920s when her dress caught fire whilst looking in a mirror over the mantelpiece .

Flooding

The Fire Brigade was often called out to deal with flooding. The *Royal Ferry Hotel*, New Brighton and old *Seacombe Ferry Hotel's* cellars were vulnerable to high tides and the Brigade would be called to pump the water out. Heavy rains would cause flooding in Liscard Village and the Brigade would be paid to pump the water from the cellars of Jones' Garage and the *Royal Oak* public-house.

Hoses

Fire Brigades have used different types of hoses over the years. The old canvas hoses would puncture if a vehicle was driven over but could be repaired using a copper rivet. Some hoses were rubber-lined. The later canvas hoses would swell with the flax and seal any holes thus becoming watertight again. Many accidents happened when a Fireman was fighting a fire with a squirt on top of a ladder and would fall off due to a vehicle driving over the hose. Later a simple invention allowed the hose to lie between hose-wraps thus enabling a vehicle to drive over them without affecting the pressure. Modern hoses can now be driven over.

In later years, hoses were made of nylon which were lighter than the old type, but were no use in grass fires as the embers could burn the cover. Special wraps were used to hold the hose while the Fireman was working on a ladder to prevent the pressure hauling him off.

The Firemen would remain at a fire until the last flames were extinguished and after a large fire would stay on to damp it down using hoses.

In 1928, the Wallasey Brigade decided that new hose was necessary. Five lengths of 100ft. were purchased from George Angus and Co. Ltd. which cost £412.5s.0d and another order was placed with R Reddasway for the same amount at £8.10s.0d a length. Ceiling Hooks would be used to make a hole in the ceiling so that a further inspection could be carried out.

The Wallasey Fire Brigade always took part in local parades. During one parade PC Gallagher kept his eye on all the coins collected from the public, using long canes with nets attached to the end, in aid of local hospitals. On the Engine was driver Bert Clague, Bert Winstanley and others. Sometimes they would use an upturned umbrella to catch the coins. Bert Clague went on to become a Sergeant with Regent Street Fire Station, Cambridge (he was brother-in-law to Herbert Winstanley).

******

Moreton

When there was a Call-Out to Moreton on a bitterly cold night, the men's hands would freeze as they held on to the rail on the Fire Engine. Quite often when they arrived they found that the Birkenhead Brigade were already there and had put the flames out so there was nowhere for the Wallasey crew to warm their hands! This was the time when there was rivalry between the Brigades and they would try to beat each other to the fire. They were glad to get back home where their wives had a hot drink of cocoa ready for them.

On 1 April, 1928 the Parish of Moreton and a section of the Parish of Bidston were added to the Borough of Wallasey (Saughall Massie and parts of the Parishes of Bidston and Upton were added in 1933).

The area was subject to flooding on account of low-lying ground. In the days before the World War Two, parts of Moreton were known as 'Shanty Town' on account of the wooden bungalows. When there was heavy rain, the area was completely covered with water. Men and boys rolled up their trousers and took off their boots and socks and waded through the water and the girls hitched up their skirts and paddled about in bare feet. Summer camping was very popular in Moreton. Some campers had their tents better prepared than others with wooden planks on the floor, table and chairs and an oil stove for cooking. Very often these would be marooned by the floods. Old caravans, tramcars or railway wagons were used as holiday homes. Other wooden bungalows were erected on stilts, such as those in field of the Fellowship House under the management of Mrs. Eleanor Burden. With the shortage of housing, a lot of them became permanent homes in the early nineteen twenties. Sanitation was a concern for the local authority and when Wallasey Corporation took over responsibility for Moreton, they took measures to rectify the problem by condemning most of the temporary buildings and building new houses.

Better roads and drains have curtailed the problem today, but there is still occasional flooding and the Brigade is then called out to deal with the situation.

******

'Leaping Lena'

The old Leyland-Mather & Platt motor pump was still in use. It was christened 'Leaping Lena' by the Firemen due to the fact that it would leapt forward when put into gear and the clutch let in. It was also unpredictable when cranking the engine.

All the controls were duplicated at the rear of the Fire Engine. The throttle was also at the rear so that when the pump was running, one could control the speed of the engine. On one occasion whilst going to a fire in Moreton, the engine raced ahead and Ginger Whitfield had great difficulty in driving it. The trouble turned out to be that the throttle had been pulled out at the rear controls and one of the men had to climb to the back and push it in.

The Fire Engine was in use until 1952.

Motorcycle

In October 1930 the Council agreed to the Watch Committee's proposal to the purchase of a 9.86 Horse Power BSA motorcycle with special sidecar chassis for the conveyance of the Portable Motor Pump. It cost £102.15s.0d with the Pump having been purchased earlier for £165. It was for use in Moreton.

The Registration Number HF 278 of another vehicle was transferred to the motor cycle in 1930.

A fire broke out on 30 December 1931 at the *Lyceum Electric Palace* Cinema, which is seen on the right in Egremont

Loss of good men

Tragedy struck Fireman Bob Jones' family when his daughter, Thelma, and her husband were killed in an accident whilst on holiday abroad. Bob lost other members of his family through illness and he, himself, died as a result of the fire at the Town Hall due to inhaling smoke as there were no smoke masks at that period. On 24 November 1928 Sergeant Thomas Wilkinson died of pneumonia after catching a chill due to getting wet while attending a fire. He was a popular member of the Brigade, devoted to his duty being known for his unfailing humour and geniality. He became a Sergeant in the Wallasey Brigade in 1923 coming from the Sheffield Fire Brigade which he joined in 1911. He was a sportsman having played football with Vale of Lune and Halton FC. He was also a keen swimmer taking part in the Annual River Swim from Woodside to New Brighton. He was a Freemason and a member of Egremont Lodge 2872. Neither Thomas nor his wife, had wanted a formal funeral although he was entitled to one as a Sergeant. However, members of the Lodge attended along with a contingent of Firemen from Sheffield under Sergeant Tether. Wallasey Fire Brigade were represented by Firemen Benfield, Cash, Evason, Maddocks, Marsden and Thorley. His widow received a Police Widow's Pension of £30 per annum and £10 per annum for each of his two children. She also received an extra £10 for Tom's service to the Force.

There was also much sadness among the men and neighbours over the death of Tommy Highton who lived at 29 Manor Road. In the course of his Fireman's career, he could have served for a period as Deputy Fire Chief.

Vote For Us

In 1931, the residents of Upton were given the choice of becoming part of Wallasey or Birkenhead.

On the morning prior to the poll, a Wallasey Fire Engine drove around the neighbourhood displaying placards with the wording "We can reach a fire in Upton in 10 minutes".

The Birkenhead Brigade responded in the afternoon with an engine carrying the message "Why wait 10 minutes to have your fire put out when we can do it in four". Birkenhead won the poll 2401 to 661.

******

Cinema Fire

The *Lyceum Electric Palace* cinema, Egremont, caught fire on 30 December 1931. A passer-by noticed flames through the windows and summoned the Fire Brigade by breaking the glass of the Fire Alarm opposite the Cinema and pulling the lever. There were about six of these alarms situated around the town. By the time the Brigade got there the cinema was well alight and all that was saved was the projection suite. There had been a couple of previous fires at the cinema; first was in 1930 when there was a fire in a store room and another one five months later when the balcony had to be closed on account of the damage.

The cinema was eventually demolished in March 1933 and replaced with the new *Gaumont Palace* cinema. During the process of removing the rubble, workmen found a number of old coins, newspapers and documents that had been placed in a canister dating from the time of the laying of the foundation stone of the old Presbyterian Church that originally stood on the site.

The beautiful new cinema opened on Monday 13 November 1933 with the showing of the film "I was a Spy". This cinema ,which became the six-screen *Apollo*, closed down May 2000 due to a fall in audience numbers and also the opening of the new *Warner Village* cinema in Conway Park, Birkenhead.

******

Fire Alarms

The standard Fire Alarm of the time was a box mounted on a stout pillar about six feet from the ground. They could be found at Albion Street, Birkenhead Road, Grove Road, King Street, Magazine Lane, Mainwaring Road, Mill Lane, Poulton Road, Rowson Street and one in Wallasey Village. The door of the boxes could be opened with a key and were tested regularly. The idea was that when the Fire Brigade was needed a person would break the glass, pull the lever and wait for the Brigade to arrive. Then tell the Firemen where the fire was. When the telephone become more popular these were used less and eventually replaced with the Police Pillar from which one could call the Fire Brigade, Police or Ambulance by telephone.

In the year ending 31 March 1931 there were 88 fire calls with only three False Alarms. Over £17,000 worth of property was damaged. The Brigade cost £6,088.9s.4d to maintain compared with £6,021.6s.2d the previous year. The Ambulance was called out to attend some 657 road accidents (an increase of 156 over the previous year) and they made 774 private patient journeys. They also took care of 395 cases for the Assistance Committee and in transported 294 prisoners to and from various places. 41 bodies had to be collected from the foreshore and other places within the Borough Boundary. In addition to transporting patients and prisoners, the Brigade had to round-up mad dogs and employing their trade skills (a trade qualification was an essential condition of recruitment) upon favoured Councillors' private property.

The cost of running the Fire Brigade in 1932 was £5,680.

The Brigade answered some 108 Call-outs in 1933, of which 11 were False Alarms. Resulting from the fires, there was £1,150 worth of damage. The cost of running the Fire Brigade in that year was £5,289, which compared with £5,680 for the previous year.

The Ambulance made 991 journeys with private patients and the service was called out to 658 road accidents. There were 410 cases dealt with for the Public Assistance Committee. The Ambulance also carried some 291 prisoners to Courts or prisons and 44 bodies had to be collected from the foreshore and elsewhere. So one realises just how important the Fire Brigade were in those days.

In 1934 the Brigade were called out 66 times to deal with fires in which 13 were False Alarms. Fires were responsible for £3,952 worth of damage. The Ambulance attended 596 road accidents. As many as 36 bodies were taken from the sands and other places. The Personnel consisted of one Inspector, one Sergeant and twelve Fire Constables. To maintain the Brigade cost over £5,500 of ratepayers' money.

Nationally, there were only 4,272 professional Firemen by the mid 1930s and nearly half were members of the London Fire Brigade.

The New Leyland 'Cub'

In 1935 the Wallasey Fire Brigade purchased a Leyland KF4 'Cub' Pump. This 27 HP Fire Engine was fitted with an Ajax ladder and searchlight which was fastened above the bell. It had a 40 gallon tank and carried a spare wheel on the outside next to the driver. The 'Braidwood' body was designed so the crew sat outwards on either side of the vehicle and the Station Officer sat next to the driver. Crowbars and an assortment of tools as well as hose and breathing equipment were carried in lockers. The old smoke helmets had a 50ft. air line that was connected to a hand bellows unit that had to be placed well away from the smoke infested air. This Fire Engine was one of the most popular pumps that was in use at the Fire Station. I think it is still in existence. However, when it first arrived at the Fire Station there were no side ladders and it was a considerable time before these were delivered.

The Leyland Fire Engines were not fast revving and the pump would slowly thump away as it pumped the water.

In 1935 there were 84 Call Outs, of which nine were False Alarms.

This photograph was taken of the Leyland FK4 'Cub' Pump and Ajax ladder with the crew. Left to Right: Fireman E Phillips, Fireman L Pugh, Driver Bill Hughes, Fireman W Forber and Section Leader Norman Newton

The amount of fire damage amounted to £3,672. A fire occurred at the varnish works of James A Kemp and Co near Seacombe Ferry on 15 June 1935 when the building was destroyed.

The Ambulance was called to 666 road accidents and they made 1,264 journeys with patients. They also ferried some 243 prisoners and made 647 cases for the Public Assistance Committee. As many as 31 bodies had been found on the foreshore and other places and these had been taken to the mortuary.

The Fire Brigade, which had a staff of 14, cost the ratepayers about five and a half thousand pounds.

There were 80 Call-Outs for the Brigade in 1937, of which 13 proved to be False Alarms. About £1,900 worth of damage was caused to property. The Ambulance was kept busy in transporting 1,637 patients and 638 people involved in road accidents. Some 77 prisoners were removed and there were some 694 cases conveyed for the Public Assistance Committee. In addition there were 38 bodies which had to be collected from the foreshore and elsewhere. A new Ambulance was added to the fleet that carried the town's Coat of Arms on the side. There was an older one that had a white roof. The cost to the ratepayers for running the Brigade year ending 31 March 1937 was £6,679.

Councillor George Reakes was convinced that war with Germany was coming and he warned cinema audiences. A film entitled "The Gap" was shown at the Gaumont Palace, King Street. It depicted a town after an air-raid. George spoke after it had been screened saying "If a war breaks out, Wallasey will be bombed and our town will resemble the film you have just seen."

He went on to encourage men to join the Air-Raid Wardens and the AFS without delay; he joined the ARP in 1938.

A lot of people in the town were saying "Reakes is going crackers. He has become a complete warmonger." But how right he was with his warnings.

The Air-Raid Precautions Act of 1937 made local authorities recruit and train a volunteer force of Auxiliaries to supplement the peacetime Brigades. By the 1 September 1939 the AFS had enrolled 89,000 Auxiliaries and 6,000 women, meaning that the regular Firemen were out numbered. Most of these enrolled into the Fire Brigade Union. From 3,500 members in 1939 it rose to 66,500 in 1940 of which 1,000 were women.

Seacombe Tragedy

The Wallasey Fire Brigade received a Call-Out at 9.14am on Saturday 3 December 1938. The Fire Engine, under the supervision of Sergeant Holt, arrived at the house in Hawthorne Grove four minutes later.

Mrs Worthington, had left her two children, Peter, aged three years and Annette, 19 months, alone in the house. She had often left them in the house while she ran to the shop to get meat and would quickly run back. However, on this occasion she returned home and was horrified to see smoke coming out of the window. She cried out for help and an elderly gentleman Thomas George Jackson, a retired Corporation employee from Clarendon Road, heard her cries and came running. He fell to his knees to avoid the flames and crawled in. He grabbed hold of Peter who was by the door and passed the child to the waiting neighbours.

Thinking that the baby was upstairs, he, and other men, tried to put out the flames with buckets of water. When Sergeant Holt arrived, he was told that the baby was in one of the bedrooms. He dashed upstairs but could not find the child. He ordered his men to drag some burning furniture into the street. The settee and chair were both blazing. When they pulled the chair away, the body of the burned baby fell away. Annette had died immediately and Peter died three days later in hospital.

At the inquest, the Coroner highly praised Mr Jackson for his bravery and his name would go forward for recognition. He was later presented with a framed certificate by Mr RT Highnet, the Wallasey Coroner, on behalf of the Liverpool Shipwreck and Humane Society.

Sergeant Holt said that the fire could have been caused when pyjamas had fallen from the rail above the fire grate. Mr John Worthington said that the fire guard around the grate had been properly fastened and was still in position after the fire. It was reported that most of the burns to the baby had been caused after death.

The funeral took place on the following Wednesday at St Paul's Church where the first part of the service took place. Councillor George Reakes attended the service. Also present was Mr Jackson whose heroic efforts at the fire had won general admiration. The Mayor of Wallasey, Councillor Arthur Frank Pullen, wrote him a letter in appreciation of his gallant action. He had known Mr Jackson for many years, both being members of the Seacombe Brotherhood.

******

1938

From morn to afternoon -
From afternoon to night.

WS Gilbert

In 1938, Mr Nicholson had a Deputy in Sgt. Joseph Holt and 12 Police/Firemen. Among the Firemen were Bob Herron, Jack Williams, Bob Jones, Herbert Winstanley, Harold Cash, Jack 'Gunner' Marshall, Len Marsden, Richard Webster and Jack Beech. Another member of the Wallasey Brigade was Joe Holdsworth who came from Blackburn as Sergeant.

There were 100 Auxiliary Firemen to man the 14 power pumps which formed part of the mobile Fire Brigade to patrol the borough in time of emergency in addition to the normal Fire Brigade equipment and personnel. Men had to be trained and the equipment kept in tip-top condition and it was necessary to have further buildings for storage of the machines and suitable room for lectures. At the end of the year, there were 50 fully-trained Auxiliary Firemen and a further 150 still receiving training, including 20 hours' training in anti-gas measures, taking 60 hours for each man to complete the course.

A further 100 recruits were waiting for training.

The men were divided into two watches, 'A' and 'B'. Each Watch had about 20 men with two Sub-Officers and two Leading Firemen. A 'C' Watch was added later. The Duty Board gave the names of the Firemen and what Appliance they were to man.

When Duty Hours came in they consisted of a 60 hour week. Six days on, followed by 24 hours off then five nights of 15 hours followed, then back on days. On Sundays, the Firemen were on duty for 24 hours. Two days off and one standby, which all the men got. Change-over was on Sundays - a day and a night (24 hours) when another watch came on. The 24 hours on Sunday would take the men automatically on to nights. In each watch there would be groups of four or six men. Four would get Monday and Tuesday off. The next four got Tuesday, Wednesday as an overlap providing there was full manning. Five men on each Engine-five on the Pump Escape, five on the Major and five on the Light. There would be a couple of spare men. In all, seventeen or eighteen men on duty. Even the men who were off duty were expected to stay in the proximity of the Fire Station and should one want to go farther afield he was obliged to inform the Sergeant of his precise whereabouts in case of emergencies. Each Brigade had a Fire Prevention Officer who made regular visits to public places and was always on hand to offer advice on the subject.

Each year, a Government Inspector would come to inspect the Brigade. He would first book himself into the Seacombe Ferry Hotel, have a shower and a drink. Then he would telephone to call a Test Turnout to the hotel, time them and carry out an inspection. During the year 1938, the Brigade received 113 calls as well as 12 False Alarms. The damage to property was estimated at £7,633.

The cost of running the Fire Brigade in the year ending 31 March 1938 came to £.5,599 against the previous year of £6,679. The Ambulance had been called out 626 times to road accidents and they had also made 2,022 journeys with patients.

They were still using the Service for transporting prisoners and 133 were conveyed. They also carried out nearly 700 cases for the Public Assistance.

The Ambulance collected some 53 bodies from the shore and other places.

All the Firemen had to be qualified in First Aid as they also did Ambulance Duty. The ambulances were used to take patients to and from hospital and as far as Deva, Chester. Of the two ambulances that were kept at the Central Fire Station, one could be used as a Police Black Maria when needed.

A telephone alarm system was set up in various parts of the Borough.

When one of the Fire Engines needed attention or repairing, it was carried out at the Fire Station by the mechanic after which one of the men would take great delight in putting it through its paces around the town.

Mr Nicholson had become Fire Chief straight from Civvy Street into uniform and it must have been difficult for him. The men made allowances for him as he could be quite trying at times. He would treat the men like children. Anything that happened he would call all the men out – even those who were off duty, and speak to them about the matter. He was a keen disciplinarian.

On seeing an Appliance out of place he would say to the Police Sergeant, "Get the men on parade".

The Sergeant would press the bell that was connected to all the houses and the men would come on parade and the Fire Chief would come out of his office and ask "Where is Fireman So and So?" "He is off duty, sir", answered the Sergeant. "Get him out." All this was due to the fact that a Pump was out of position. No one remarked on the minor complaint. No answering back. They bit their tongue and tolerated these sort of irritations as not all jobs gave a pension on retirement. Nevertheless, Mr Nicholson

was a very good Fire Chief and was a likeable gentleman who got on well with both his officers and men.

Although Mr Nicholson was a local Methodist Lay Preacher, he allowed the men an occasional ten minute break for a drink of beer in the *Royal Oak,* opposite the Fire Station. If one of them was late back he would forfeit his next visit to the pub.

On another occasion, there was a Portable Hand Pump which had brass handles left by the back door . This Pump was used for farm fires and could be carried across the fields in order to get water from a pond or river. The Pump was left out of place and Mr Nicholson came in from the bright sunshine and caught his knee cap against one of the brass handles. He was so annoyed that he called all the men out to find out who left it out of place.

Fireman Herbert Winstanley used to chop the sticks to light the boiler for the central heating at the Fire Station. Mr Nicholson would take some of these chips home for his fire but once they were too large and would not fit the grate. The men were called out and he asked who had chopped the sticks. Herbert said he had done so. He was ticked off. "Well you know that they have to be six inches long and a half an inch wide."

Although Mr Nicholson was known as 'Billy Nick' by the men they always addressed him as 'sir' and when referring to him to another officer would call him 'Mr Nicholson'.

Mr Walter Meacock

And I'm never, never sick at sea!
What never?
No never
What NEVER?
Hardly ever!"

WS Gilbert

Walter Meacock who was a plumber by trade, joined the Brigade in 1938 and was made a Sub-Officer as he was a leader in the Sea Scouts and had spent all his life swimming or sailing in the river. With the war approaching it would be necessary to have Fire Boats and he was the right person for the job. (At the time of writing this grand 93 year-old gentleman is enjoying life in a nursing home in New Brighton It was a pleasure to meet such a perfect gentleman and is one of the last of the Old Brigade.)

One of his first jobs was to help with the distribution of gas masks to the people of Wallasey.

For she IS such a smart little craft -
Such a neat little, sweet little craft -
Such a bright little -
Tight little -
Light little -
Trim little, slim little craft!

WS Gilbert

The Brigade took charge of a small Fireboat, which was not unlike a fishing-smack and it was kept in the Station Yard, by the old Slaughter House. There, the men overhauled it and after they had de-clinkered it, they set about painting it. Eventually, the boat was taken down to the docks and lowered into the water.

There it did a round trip. All was satisfactory. Then it was tied up next to a ship. The large vessel listed and leaned on the Fire-Boat, sinking it – that was the end of the Fireboat.

Other Fireboats that were in the docks included the *Destiny* which had been a private motor-launch and boasted three bathrooms and central heating.

Another one was the *Ut Norling* which was originally a lifeboat and had a Morris engine. The Scandinavian name translated meant

Mr Walter Meacock, taken in the nursing/rest home, wearing the old brass helmet

'Out North'.

Ted Colpin had been a seafarer and he joined the NFS and was on the Fireboats that were in the docks, one being at the East Quay. There were about a dozen or more fireboats on Merseyside as the war progressed. Training Head Quarters was in the West Float Dock with Walter Meacock in charge. One day a large van arrived with a load of anti-freeze and the fellow asked how many gallons of water there were in the dock. That question was unanswerable so it was just poured into the dock. I do not suppose it had any effect.

John Clitheroe of the NFS Head Quarters in Mill Lane, West Derby, Liverpool wrote to Walter Meacock and his crew of the *Destiny* congratulating them on the rescue of Fireman Neilson from the Mersey, who had fallen overboard whilst helping to free the fouled anchor. He had been carried down river in the darkness and when he had surfaced had the presence of mind to use his battery-operated torch. He signalled and then it went out due to the water. Keeping calm, he unscrewed the bottom, emptied out the water and switched on – it gave just one more flash then went out but luckily he was spotted and rescued.

One day Walter was out checking the hydrants in Moreton and after completing about a half of dozen was approached by a Policeman and asked "Are you in charge?"

"Yes", replied Walter.

"I've just had a lady out complaining that her washing has gone all rusty red because of this."

It turned out that the lady was his wife and his checking of the mains had disturbed the rust in the pipes!

Walter Meacock retired from the Fire Service as Station Officer.

******

Second World War

Chief Constable John Ormerod, as ARP Controller, was Director of Fire Services of the borough .

By 1939, under Mr Nicholson, the Brigade had a Pump-Escape and two Pumps, all being Leylands, with 15 full-time staff and a number of Police Volunteers. Mr. Donning was Senior Company Officer and Company Officer was George Mercer.

The staff had been increased and equipment had been supplied by the Home Office for use of the Auxiliary Units.

The Fire Brigade cost £5,417 in the year ending 31 March 1939 compared with £5,599 for the previous year.

Like the rest of the country, church bells were silent and only rung should there be an invasion.

At the outbreak of war in September 1939, there were 120 separate Fire Brigades in Britain with each Brigade operating independently. The AFS had been formed in 1938 with the Secretary of State at the Home Office in charge of some 1,500 brigades in Great Britain. A total of 400 members of the Auxiliary Fire Service were enrolled as full-time Firemen. A number of the younger men had joined the Forces so the Fire Service had enlisted civilians and these men had to be trained with some of the original men being quickly promoted. The NFS became a reserved occupation and those men who had joined the Forces could return to the Fire Service if they so wished. Many of the trained young men were called up to go into the Army and it was being realised that these men would be better back home fighting fires.

Firemen were taught to avoid heroics and the saving of another life was the only justification for risking his own. They were to face many dangers and long hours of fighting fires caused by enemy bombs, whilst under continuous attack. The AFS men were unpaid volunteers who came from all walks of life with many of them having jobs during the day and coming on duty at night after work.

Chief Constable John Ormerod, as ARP Controller was Director of Wallasey Fire Service, is seen with the King and Queen

31

The Blackout came into force and one of its many victims was 75 year-old Lawrence Law of Green Lane who was knocked down by a motor car on 5 October 1939 during the Black-Out and was killed instantly.

On Sunday 31 March 1940 a large scale test of Wallasey's Civil Defence took place with almost 2,000 being engaged. A mock Air-Raid was staged and fires were lighted in various parts of the town which were quickly dealt with. The exercise was watched by the Mayor and members of the Emergency Committee.

It is interesting to note that as from 1 May 1940 Mr Herbert Winstanley, OBE was appointed Chief Constable of Liverpool and Director of their Fire Brigade. He served in the Liverpool Police for 33 years but was not related to the Winstanley family of Wallasey.

The Brigade cost £5,656 to maintain for the year ending 31 March 1940. They had been called out 111 times and they had prevented over £133,500 worth of property from being burnt. However, there was more than £2,500 worth of damage caused.

The Ambulance, as always had been kept busy. There had been 2,197 patient journeys and they had attended 704 road accidents. Some 487 cases for the Public Assistance had been dealt with and 96 prisoners had been conveyed to and from destinations. There were 66 washed-up bodies on the beaches which had to be collected and taken to the mortuary.

The old Fire Station in Brougham Road was reopened.

Whenever bombs fell, more often than not fires resulted which meant that the Firemen's resources were called upon.

Seven high explosive bombs were dropped on Wallasey in August 1940, followed by further air-raids and the Fire Service had to deal with the resulting fires. At times there were so many that obtaining water was difficult especially when large number of the borough's water mains had been fractured. One of the answers was for water to be brought in from inland Brigades in water carriers. Another was to set up EWS (Emergency Water Supply) tanks in various parts of the town to be used in emergency to combat fires including one on the corner of Manor Road and Belgrave Street and another

in Imperial Avenue and one being by the side of the Egremont Presbyterian (now the Manor Church Centre) at the Seabank Road end of Manor Road. Most of them were rectangle but a few were circular. These tanks would attract children who would take the opportunity to sail their little boats. In St George's Park there was a sunken canvas EWS reservoir. This was filled by taking water from the boating lake, along the promenade, up Tollemache and Hope Streets, up Rowson Street to St George's Park. Wallasey had two water supplies (there were also wells in Seaview Road), Leasowe Road and another by the Penny Bridge. Both of these later suffered bomb damage. Water was pumped from the West Float to Central Park lake by hose. When water had to be pumped from long distances, several relay pumps would be deployed.

The Fire Brigade Division of the Home Office had supplied 35 pumps of various types, twelve Water Dams, either of steel or canvas, 70 Extension Ladders and a large amount of hose. There was also a large selection of branch pipes and nozzles. The Dam Unit consisted of a canvas dam supported on a frame on a flat-bedded lorry. Heavy Pump Units were to pump water in relays.

There was a delay in building the Fire Station Extension, as the Home Office had not given their approval. However, by 1940 there were eight Auxiliary Fire Stations in the borough, which were manned day and night. Out of the total of 500 Auxiliary Firemen, over 400 were part-time. Mr Colin Sanders was appointed Commandant who was assisted by Mr Stafford Donning as his Deputy who worked alongside Inspector Nicholson, the Fire Chief, and his staff.

Folk gathered to read the names of those who had been killed in the raids which were pinned to a notice board outside the Town Hall.

During the past year, the Fire Brigade had been called out 81 times of which 24 were False Alarms. They saved property to the value of about £387,000 albeit the fires caused £12,700 worth of damage. The Ambulance had been called out to 629 road accidents in the year and they had conveyed over two and a half thousand patients.

Below: *Members of the Wallasey NFS in a wartime pose*

In addition there were over 500 cases conveyed for the Public Assistance Committee and 82 prisoners had been transported. The figure for the removal of bodies from the foreshore and other places was still high at 42. Mr Stafford Donning who was an excellent leader, became Commander of the Auxiliaries with Mr George Mercer his Deputy.

Concrete pyramids were placed along the sandhills at Leasowe and elsewhere and other precautions were made should the Germans land from the Irish Sea.

As regards Fort Perch Rock New Battery, the shipping channels were protected by two six-inch guns. There were also four searchlights of six million candlepower. Seaforth Battery was on the other side of the river and in addition there were the sea minefield and the torpedo tubes on the landing stage at New Brighton Ferry.

The first gun shots of the war were fired from Fort Perch Rock when some residents thought it was the one o'clock gun. Some 15 minutes after the declaration of war, the battery fired two 6-inch shells from No.2 gun across the bow of a fishing boat that was entering the closed Rock Channel. Captain Charles Cocks was in command of the Fort (he later became Colonel). They also opened fire on what was thought to be an enemy submarine.

The Army had taken over "Cliff Villa" in Wellington Road and 4.5 guns were mounted in the grounds.

Is London to be wrecked?
What are we to expect?
What danger is at hand?
Let us understand
What danger is at hand!

WS Gilbert

One of the first Call-Outs in the war was on 10 August 1940 following the raid which started at about 12.30am. Seven High Explosive bombs were dropped on Wallasey. Two enemy bombs fell at Stroude's Corner, Brighton street [this air-raid is mentioned in the Part 1 which is devoted to the Wallasey Police]. A fire followed which was confined to one shop and the regular Fire Brigade arrived along with the AFS and fought the flames for an hour. Other bombs fell on Adelaide Street, Cliff Road, East Street, Field Road, Florence Cottages, Gorsey Lane, Ingleby Road, Linwood Road, Lily Grove, Mill Lane, Rake Lane, Palatine Road, and St George's Mount. Eleven High Explosive Bombs fell on Wallasey with Property catching fire and water mains being fractured. A bomb fell by the railway embankment.

Four people were killed and four seriously injured. 32 casualties in all.

German planes dropped sea mines in the approaches to the Mersey.

On 15 August there were three warnings. Planes were heard overhead after the last warning. One would see the occasional German reconnaissance plane high in the sky probably taking aerial photographs of Merseyside. The AA guns would open fire but they failed to hit the plane. After the war, several of these photographs were recovered and it is surprising the detail they contained. Ships in the docks, warehouses and other buildings are clearly seen. There is a detailed one of Wallasey. All the roads can be easily identified and the lighthouse is marked (Leuchtturn). It was estimated that there were 150 bombers over Merseyside on the raid of 27/28 August. Incendiary Bombs were dropped with many falling in fields and causing no damage but a water main, however, was damaged.

Over 200 German aircraft attacked Wallasey and Liverpool on 30/31 August, causing much damage. The School Hall of the Wallasey High School (now Weatherhead School), Mountpleasant Road received a direct hit. The old Wallasey Municipal Buildings in

Harry Driscoll

Church Street was bombed and the Civic Hall in the Town Hall received a direct hit.

The raid of 31 August/1 September 1940, which started with a Red Alert at 23.50 and the second Red Alert at 00.22 with the All Clear given at 03.10, did a great deal of damage. It wrecked the four-manual Henry Willis organ that had once been used in the Leinster Hall in Dublin and installed in the Town Hall in 1926. This fine instrument was never replaced. Many houses were destroyed in the vicinity of Church Street. The battleship Prince of Wales suffered damage in Cammell Laird's basin when a bomb fell between ship and dock wall. She started to list as the water rushed through her damaged plates. The Birkenhead Fire Brigade were called and they pumped out thousands of gallons of water, a task that lasted two and a half days.

There was an air-raid over Moreton on 11 September 1940. Bombs fell in fields and a Centre was hit. As Wallasey Fire Service was now part of the new NFS Wallasey's Chief Fire Officer was appointed Divisional Fire Officer for the Wirral area.

Vehicles that were converted into ambulances were stationed at the YMCA. These were kept on the forecourt of the building and were manned by members of the Civil Defence (I understand that after the war, several of these people remained on to form Acorn Table Tennis Club that played in the YMCA).

There was also a Fire Guard Depot at 4/6 Hale Road.

Douglas Cooper from Marlborough Road was one of the men there and a relative of his, by the name of Frank James Cooper, had served a number of years in the Acton Fire Brigade and received a Long Service Medal from the National Fire Brigades' Association.

An AFS Post was hit on 17 September killing all the occupants. Eight lives were lost, but that figure does not correspond with the tally recorded for the month of four – due to the logistical problems then of recording all the information, much of which was strictly confidential, many conflicting reports were issued.

A Fire Engine rushed to a scene and had turned into one road and as they did so, a high-explosive bomb landed on the junction that they had just passed. A little later, they were engaged in rescuing people from a house that was on fire when an enemy plane swooped down and opened fire with their machine guns. Luckily, there were no casualties.

Brick Air-Raid Shelters were also damaged and had to be repaired. 120 people used the basement of the Town Hall as a shelter and one would see folk bedded down for the night in the basement of the New Brighton Tower where there was room for 200 with Wardens in charge. The cellars of the Maris Stella Convent were also used as a shelter as was New Brighton Bathing Pool's basement. In other parts of Merseyside, people slept on the underground railway station platforms.

There was also the problem of unexploded bombs. Some of these were not discovered until much later. One had landed in a laundry and the staff had been working on the site without knowing that it was there. People had to cook on open fires as the gas supply had been fractured in the bombing.

A van with a loud speaker informed the public where they could obtain water. Milk tanks arrived were filled with water for the general public who queued with anything that would hold water.

The electricity supply was restored and was followed by the water mains being repaired

There were nine raids in September and three in October. Small fires were quickly dealt with before they could do further damage. Birkenhead lost their world-famous *Argyle Theatre* in the September raids. A firebomb hit the roof and went on to destroy the whole theatre, save the box office.

Barrage Balloons were struck with lightening during a heavy thunderstorm while enemy planes were overhead on 1 November 1940 and on account of high winds on 12 November the Barrage Balloons were kept moored to their pads. Raiders came in at low level and the dockland suffered damage also Gorsey Lane Gas Works was hit.

There were heavy raids in Christmas week 1940. Enemy planes came over in waves with the first raid on the 20 December started at 6pm and lasted nearly 10 hours. People sang Christmas carols in the Community Shelters as the bombs fell on the town. Property to suffer damage was in Byerley Street, Elleray Park Road, Greenwood Lane, Earlston Road, Mount Pleasant Road, Shakespeare Road and Stoneby Drive.

During the raids of 20/21/22 December Wallasey suffered 119 fatalities and 91 seriously injured. Of the number killed, 13 had been elderly inmates of the Widows' Home (the William Rogers Home for Elderly Ladies) that stood on the corner of Withens Lane and Manor Road. The bomb had fractured the gas main and they had been gassed whilst they were trapped under the debris. Another record gives the number of eighteen widows who lost their lives in Home. The large old house was originally called *Manor Lodge* and had been built about 1830 and was converted into a Widows' Home in 1930.

The Fire Brigade was fighting fires all over the town as well as the Civil Defence who were also tackling the flames. The Wardens and First Aid workers as well as the Stretcher Bearers worked through the night. The Victoria Central Hospital had to be evacuated on account of the bombing. It remained closed until 13 January 1941 due to the boilers being damaged as well as the roof. Broken windows had to be boarded up before patients could be readmitted.

Rescue Parties were kept busy. A number of AFS men came to assist from Bebington. Houses were wrecked and many people went to live with relatives away from the bombing. Huge craters were to be seen in the road making them impassable. Children played in them and went about the town looking for the bright metal shrapnel to collect. A nose-cap from a shell was one of the most collectable items.

In January 1941 Chief Constable John Ormerod, while attending a Hot Pot Supper, held under the auspices of the Wallasey Central Auxiliary Fire Service at the Wallasey Police Recreation Club Rooms, said:-

"...But for a remarkable and astonishing display of courage and resource by our Firemen this County Borough of Wallasey might have been destroyed by fire. It would be difficult for anyone in authority to tabulate individual acts of gallantry for recognition, they being so numerous among our fire fighting personnel."

The Chief Fire Officer also spoke.

"You lads were simply wonderful and in refusing to stop carrying out your duties while the bombs were falling thick and fast you rendered a magnificent service to the Borough that had been placed in you by the Chief Commandant and myself" He added, "If I talk from now to Domesday I shall not adequately express my gratitude for all that was done on those fateful nights."

Two people were killed and three seriously injured in the January raids.

Sergeant Holt had done tremendous work in training the men.

The Central Fire Station in Manor Road housed four Appliances. The office and telephone switchboard and recreation room was also part of the building. A second building was erected in Liscard Crescent with five Appliance bays and cellars in 1941 on the site of the old Slaughter House. Above was a Lecture Room, Fire Protection Office and Men's Dormitory. The main building was enlarged with an extension to the office.

A second tower was added at the rear of the Central Fire Station for drying hoses and ladder practice. There was also a circular well for emergency water.

Sandbags were piled up in front of buildings as a protection to such as the Town Hall, Hospitals, Police Stations, Libraries and other public or important buildings. Air-Raid Wardens were supplied with stirrup pumps which were used to extinguish small fires. They also had long-handled shovels which they were able to pick up an Incendiary Bomb and dispose of it in a safe place or used it to throw sand over and extinguish the bombs.

Fire Watchers were sent to large buildings, some taking up positions on flat roofs to watch out for and report fire bombs.

The Rt. Hon. Lt. Colonel Moore-Brabazon, MP for Wallasey said: "There is no time to be lost. We must have, first and foremost, armies of Firefighters backed up by fire watchers. All AFS men taken into the Army must be released."

The Town Clerk also received a letter from Councillor George L Reakes, urging the return from the Services with HM Forces of all AFS trained men.

A wartime photograph was taken of an Austin Tender with 20 men and their Chief Officer in Montpellier Crescent.

Another wartime task that seems to have fallen to the Fire Brigade was the job of applying steam to the unexploded bombs so that the Bomb Disposal Squad could remove the fuse and render them harmless.

The Wallasey Ferries had their own firefighters and ambulance personnel and also their own ARP Group.

Brick Communal Air-Raid Shelters were erected in side-streets. Corrugated steel Anderson Shelters were half-buried in back gardens but some of these started to fill with rain water and had to have a concrete base at the point below ground level. Other houses had indoor steel Morrison table shelters.

Gas-masks were issued and they had to be returned to various points where an extra filter was taped on to the end of the gas-mask and there were special baby gas units.

Food rationing was the order of the day and each individual received 20 Clothing Coupons. Poorer people used to sell their clothing coupons for a pound for the twenty. Sweets and chocolates were in short supply and would be sold out within a matter of minutes of being delivered to a shop. They were later rationed and 'Personal Points' section of the Ration Book was used for the purpose.

All the eligible young men were called-up for the Army. The LDV (Local Defence Volunteers) units were set up in various parts of the town, later to be called the Home Guard. Upwards of 2,500 answered Mr Anthony Eden's appeal with many of them on duty all night and after some breakfast, would set off for their day jobs. Mr. William Duncan Taylor, JP was appointed Group Commander of the 16th Cheshire (Wallasey) Battalion.

Air-Raid Sirens were installed on the roofs of tall buildings in different parts of the town. One was on top of the Central Fire Station in Liscard Village.

Air-Raid Wardens patrolled the streets at night and knocked at the door of houses when they spotted the slightest chink of light from the blackout curtains. Barrage Balloons were seen all over the town, being usually stationed in parks. One of the Barrage Balloons broke away from its moorings in 1941 and became entangled in the tower of St James' Church, New Brighton, causing damage to the stonework. Another one escaped from a site in Liscard and men had to climb onto the roofs to gather up the cable.

There were enemy air-raids over Wallasey on 12/13/14 March 1941. Tens of thousands of Incendiary Bombs were dropped over a wide area. High Explosive Bombs and Parachute Mines were driven by the fresh breeze and landed a mile from the docks, causing much damage to houses in the town. Marymount Convent was bombed and the Victoria Central Hospital was damaged with patients having to be evacuated due to a breakdown in electricity, gas and water supplies. Church Street, which was once a very elegant district with large houses, was wrecked with nothing but ruins on either side of the street.

Within less than two hours of the first attack, the main water supply in Leasowe Road was fractured on 12 March causing complete failure of water which greatly effected the work of the Firefighters and water had to be taken from the docks, river and the EWS tanks that were sited in various places in the Borough.

The canvas Water Dams mounted on lorries proved to be useful. Some fires remained unchecked for nearly two days.

In the March Blitz the *Coliseum Cinema* in Wallasey Village received a direct hit, causing a fire and due to the damage had to be demolished soon afterwards. The cinema was rebuilt after the war and was called the *Phoenix* at the cost of £40,000 (It closed as a cinema in 1983 and was demolished in 1988).

The old house that stood in Breck Road that was called *Darley Dene* (formally known as *The Slopes*) had been requisitioned by the Army at the outbreak of the war and used as barracks and HQ. During a heavy air-raid the house received a direct hit from a land mine that was intended for the docks 12 March 1941 resulting in the death of 17 soldiers and a number of injured men. The old mansion had been built for Thomas Monk of Monk and Newall, the contractors who had constructed the Great Float Docks and the Ferry Approaches of 1878. Mr Bewley lived there in 1845. After the bombing, the ruin was then used as a training ground for the Civil Defence and NFS. A fire would be started and the men would be trained in how to extinguish the flames with use of the stirrup pump. They also carried out other training work. It remained in a ruinous state for some years. Youngsters played there and it was not until 1959 that the house was demolished.

Some of these soldiers had just put out a fire in the kitchen of *Bird's House* on the corner of Limekiln Lane and Poulton Bridge Road that had been caused by a fire bomb. This old house, really called *The Old House*, has always been recognised as the oldest house in Wallasey and was built in the 1600s. It survived the bombing and stills stands today.

The Gandy Belt factory received three direct hits, first in the general factory and then two bombs in the lining department but luckily there were no fatal casualties.

The first Red Alert on the 12th was at 19.13 and the All Clear soon after. The second Red Alert was at 20.29. During the evening 33 year-old Tom Roberts, who was a member of the AFS was busy urging friends and neighbours to get into the shelters, was seriously injured in the early hours of the next day when a land mine fell on Wimbledon Street and Lancaster Avenue. He died later in the day at the Cottage Hospital on 13 March 1941. His

Wartime Firemen in Monpellier Crescent, posing infront of their Austin Utility vehicle

wife, Ada, did not find out until the next day. Tom was a painter and decorator by trade and had been only married for six years and had a two year-old son named Geoff. The house they lived in at 18 Wimbledon Street which had been nicely decorated, was flattened. Ada had gone into one of the Community Air-Raid Shelters that were in the street. The land mine destroyed the four shelters killing all the occupants in one. Those who were in the end section where Ada was, also perished. The only ones left were three mothers that were in the centre. They each had a child on their knee and were surrounded with rubble and dust was everywhere. They waited and then heard rescue workers pulling bricks fallen bricks away. A man wearing a tin hat shone his torch and climbed in. "Good God", he cried," there are people alive in here!". 29 year-old Ada, her two neighbours, Mrs Blakemore and Mrs. Gibson and their children were hauled out of the wreckage. The latter lost her husband in the raid.

Ada was helped to another shelter that was still intact but she decided to leave with the others who had gone to the Memorial Hall, Manor Road. She wandered down towards the *Gaumont Cinema* and was met by a red Fire Brigade Van whose driver was an old friend with Bill Roberts, her brother-in-law, in the back. They had been going around the town switching off the water mains so they drove Ada and her young son to her mother's home in Gladstone Road. After the war, Ada remarried.

On 13 March there were thirty water dams used, as the water pressure was poor. Bombs dropped and more fires broke out including Marks and Spencer's store in Liscard Road. The Brigade had to use relays of water from the lake in Central Park by the linking up of four pumps. The Firemen were unable to save the store but the adjoining properties were saved. The building was destroyed (Marks and Spencer reopened at a later date in Coronation Buildings, Wallasey Road before returning to their former site. The building is now occupied by Primark).

On the third night, all the dams had been refilled and the Fire Service and Air-Raid Wardens were ready but the raid was not severe and all was under control.

Approximately 300 Firemen and equipment had been deployed from cities and towns in Lancashire, Cheshire and North Wales and the Controller had nothing but praise for these men.

The Regional Fire Officer, Mr George Oakes, had rendered his best when the town most needed it.

The tank on top of the Water Tower was destroyed by fire on 12 March.

Rank's and Buchanan's at Seacombe were bombed and fires resulted. Rank's Mill, by the Graving Dock, received a direct hit and it smouldered for two or three months as the heat was contained under the huge pile of bricks and flour. These formed a sort of lid that prevented the water reaching the fire. The water was taken from the dock and damping down procedures had to be deployed. A similar fire in Birkenhead Dock Road ended in the same way. The NFS were kept busy with reinforcements being sent to Wallasey and Birkenhead. Liverpool sent a foam compound to Wallasey and a TL was also despatched during night raids.

39 year-old AFS Fireman, George Harrison of Ivor Road, had been seriously injured during an air-raid, died later in the Cottage Hospital on 13 March 1941.

On Saturday 15 March some 50 Royal Engineers arrived and they soon got to work in laying a pipe track from the West Float Dock at Poulton which ran along the gutters of the roads to the lake in Central Park and to a 5,000 gallon dam in Liscard Crescent.

During these March raids there had been four major fires, eleven serious fires and some 239 fires of a lesser degree.

When a party of ARP men arrived from Penmaenmawr, Herbert Winstanley asked his son, Arthur, to take them around and join

War-time poster asking for women to join the National Fire Service as full or part-time members

up with the Squad at Buchanan's Flour Mills. Arthur was in the Army and was two days late in getting back. Although the Chief Constable had given him a letter explaining what he had been doing, he still lost 14 days' pay.

The Jump-sheet was used by the AFS in practise when men would jump off the flat roof at the Fire Station and be caught in the sheet below. The practice however was dangerous, inasmuch as those holding the sheet would look up at the men above and as they tried to position the sheet, they would pull this way and that in order to catch the falling man. It resulted in the poor fellow hitting the ground. The Jump-Sheet was abandoned and the Firemen were taught the 'Fireman's Lift'. A person could be carried down a ladder and at the same time have a free hand to hold to the side of the ladder. One man would lean over the other's shoulder and be taken down. The Firemen used the Bus Sheds' roof in Seaview Road (now the site of Asda) to practise the Escape Ladder. Herbert Winstanley (III) was carried down. Then he was approached by another Fireman who said, "You're a joiner and used to ladders and I'm a painter so we'll carry each other down."

Hook ladders were often used at fires but these could prove to be dangerous.

The AFS had been established in 1937 and there were over 600 men in the Wallasey AFS during the war.

The National Fire Service Observer Section was set up and the Water Tower in Mill Lane was used by the ARP as an observation post for fire watching.

Youths played their part too. Teenagers Michael Wilding, Sydney Pope and Harry Reid were among the numbers who volunteered to became messengers for the ARP and the NFS. As soon as the

Siren went, Harry Reid would jump on his bike and ride to the Fire Station in Manor Road to await orders. He would watch out for fires from the top of the tower.

The Derby Pool, which had opened in 1932, was bombed and the wall of the pool breached becoming unusable. The officials thought it should be used as a recreation pool for the War Workers in the town and so the wall was repaired. The pool needed filling and Fire Brigade, using three fireboats, filled it with sea water at high tide.

When King George VI and Queen Elizabeth came to Wallasey (already mentioned in Part One) to see the damage caused by enemy air-raids, the Royal Party travelled by car from Birkenhead and paid a visit to an Auxiliary Fire Service Station, seeing the appliances and personnel that had been in action on several occasions putting out fires in the town.

Harry Johnson, the haulage and sand merchant, was in the NFS and two of his 'Rio' wagons were used as water carriers. Large canvas tanks were fitted and filled with water. Harry came from Sandbach and had come to Wallasey when he delivered a Foden steam lorry to Mr. Parkinson of Mason Street. He was to explain the workings of the new lorry and Mr. Parkinson offered him a job with his company and Harry accepted. He married a local girl and settled in Wallasey. Harry Johnson was a very friendly fellow and was well-known local Methodist preacher.

Dams were set up and filled with water at Seacombe Ferry with the help of the Ferries Department. Water was also obtained from the Marine Lake in New Brighton and the Birkenhead Docks.

During raids, warehouses, churches, the Water Tower in Mill Lane, Gas Works, Electricity and shops in Liscard were set alight. All this happened whilst there was the breakdown in the water supply.

Walls and fences scaling
Promptly we appear;
Walls are unavailing,
We have entered here.

WS Gilbert

The Controller recorded that in the face of manifold difficulties the fire fighting services did all and more than was expected of them.

There was much damage to dwelling houses from High Explosive Bombs, Parachute Mines and Incendiary Bombs. During these raids, schools and churches were hit by both Incendiary Bombs and HE bombs. The gas containers in Gorsey Lane were struck and became useless as they went on fire. The Electricity Works at Poulton were hit and the Pumping Station in Seaview Road received a direct hit. According to an eye-witness, the Station had been attacked by dive-bombing. Telephone lines were down and messengers on motor cycles and pedal cycles raced around the town until lines were repaired. The roof of the GPO was damaged.

Four Rescue Parties were sent to Wallasey, two came from Heswall, one from Chester and the fourth from Hoylake but as they were coming along Marlowe Road, a bomb fell, killing two of the party and the rest were wounded with one man later dying in hospital. Over 10,000 people were homeless and cared for in Rest Centres. During the March blitz, some 2,000 gallons of hot soup and beef sandwiches were handed out.

A large number of people were homeless and had to find new places to live. Some went to live with friends or relatives locally, others moved farther afield – North Wales was a popular choice. Food canteens were sent by Major J Becke. A little later mobile canteens arrived from as far as Ashton-under-Lyne and Manchester. These were organised by Mrs Dorothy Barton and the WVS.

A work force arrived to repair property and make temporary latrines.

During the March Blitz, the Fire Service had three men killed and one Preston Fireman was drowned at the docks. Nine Wardens were also killed by the bombing.

It was found that the practice of having Pumps at the ready at various places around the town proved to be better than them patrolling around the town.

The Navy League in Withens Lane had suffered damage when a very heavy bomb landed in the grounds. The main dormitory narrowly missed a direct hit. The water main was damaged so the sailor boys had to go to get water from an emergency mobile tank in Withens Lane and queue up with their neighbours. The bomb made a huge crater that was some 60ft. across and 18 feet deep. The surrounding houses had damage to the roofs but no one was injured.

Commander HM Denny was the Officer in charge and he decided to send the boys home and were not brought back until October 1941 and on account of the dangers of air-raids, they transferred to Ravencragg in Westmoreland.

Baby of the Blitz

During a heavy air-raid over Wallasey on 12 March 1941 land mines were dropped on the town. One landed in Lancaster Avenue, killing some thirty people, most whom were in the brick Communal Shelter that was built in the middle of the road also many houses were wrecked in Wimbledon Street. After the raid, a rescue party searched for survivors and started to clear up the rubble. Bodies were laid out and covered with the Union Jack. Some three and a half days later, on Sunday morning 16 March three Rescue Workers were searching amongst the wreckage that was as high as the lampposts when he heard a faint cry. Was it a trapped cat under the pile of debris?

"What's that?", said one of the men. He thought to himself, "sounds like a cat."

He stood still and listened. He Dropped down and put his ear to the ground and listened. Again he heard a faint cry.

"Could be an animal under here", he thought. He looked up and saw seventeen year-old Norman Kendrick who was a messenger boy with the Civil Defence Corp. who had come around to see the damage.

"Give us a hand to move some of these bricks. I think there is a kitten or dog trapped under this lot. I have heard it crying. Just listen a minute."

They remained quiet and sure enough a faint cry was heard again. "That sounds like a baby!", cried the Rescue Worker.

They quickly started to remove the rubble, making sure that they did not cause more debris to fall and injure the child. Slowly but surely they got the last of the wood and bricks away. They reached down and hauled out a solid wooden Victorian cradle and there, in front of their very eyes was a four month-old baby girl covered in dust. The cradle had protected her. The parents had been killed and they seemed to have tried to protect the baby with their bodies as the mine had exploded. The rescue worker lifted the baby out of the cradle. She grabbed his thumb and began to suckle it as she had not been fed for many hours. They rendered First Aid and cleaned the baby's face then called for the ambulance, which took her to Victoria Central Hospital in Liscard where she made a full recovery. Arthur Spyzer Marriott, aged 35, and his wife Jenny, aged 33, lived at 50 Lancaster Avenue and their daughter was Irene Isabel Marriott. Rescue workers found a tin box containing £350 Savings and also securities making £844 in total which was banked for her. There was also a considerable amount of

Royal Daffodil II seen at Seacombe Stage after being sunk following an air-raid on 7 May 1941

superannuation money that was due to her father's employees, the Dock Board. Baby Irene went to live with her maternal grandparents in Wirral. She later married and is now Mrs. Foulds. Years later, the *Wallasey News* ran a series about the war and Norman Kendrick, who now lives in Moreton, wrote to the paper giving his story of the rescue and Irene was traced to Gayton. They met up for the first time since the rescue and Irene was able to thank him in person for his part in the rescue.

Surely this must be one of outstanding stories of the Home Front during the Second World War that a young baby should have survived against such odds.

14 year-old John Durrant donned his old Naval tin hat and went to help a Police Sergeant 'Bill Smiler' to hold the hose as they trained it on the flames after a large number of incendiaries had dropped on Lancaster Avenue and Wimbledon Street. The lad's father was involved in the evacuation of Dunkirk and as a Merchant Navy Captain he had been commissioned into the RNR. When he returned his dark hair had turned almost white due to the traumatic experiences and later became in command of the minesweepers in the Mersey. Fireman Herbert Winstanley was also helping in the rescue work. He got his son to come and give a hand to rescue a dog that had been trapped under rubble which they managed to free. Some time later, Bert was on the promenade and got talking to a lady who had a dog with her. She asked Bert would he like to see the dog's wounds. Yes, it was the same that he and his father had rescued from the bomb damage.

Mr Herbert Morrison, Minister for Home Security, visited the town and inspected the Wallasey Civil Defence Headquarters. He said that the Civil Defence Service was "an example to the whole country".

On the 15 March 1941, the *Mammoth,* the world's largest floating crane was sunk when hit with two bombs. Fortunately, she sank on an even keel and her great jib was undamaged. This Mersey Docks & Harbour Board's vessel was later raised and restored at a cost of £21,500.

Mines were also dropped in the West Float Dock damaging two cargo boats.

The facts for the March 1941 air-raids were as follows:-
12/13 March   20.33. to 04.02 – 209 Incidents.
13/14 March   20-37. to 02.13 – 76 Incidents.
14/15March   20.53. to 02.38 – 11 Incidents.

174 people were killed and 158 seriously injured.

There was an air-raid over Moreton on 8 April 1941 and 18 days later two parachute mines landed in a field near Bermuda Road, Moreton during the raid of 26 /27 April. One exploded causing little damage; the other was safely defused.

The first bomb to fall on Merseyside in the May Blitz of 1941, dropped on Wallasey at 10.00pm. Within minutes, there were all types of bombs falling on both sides of the Mersey in an attempt to destroy the Port of Liverpool, with the main attack falling on the Liverpool side of the river where 18 Firemen were killed and 180 injured.

The Wallasey Firemen did marvellous job in coping with the fires considering the lack of water.

A parachute mine landed on New Brighton Cricket Club's ground in Rake Lane. Many houses were wrecked all over the town and damage was widespread.

Local Wallasey artist, Mr. Grainger Smith, RCA, did an impressive painting from his home showing the Royal Liver and Mersey Docks and Harbour Board Buildings across the river silhouetted against the raging fires on 3 May. It was entitled "Enemy Action".

The port survived and carried on.

Moreton did not escape the bombing. Many houses were wrecked as a result of enemy action with property in Chapelhill Road, Carsdale Road, Fairfield Crescent, Francis Avenue and Eleanor Road all being hit.

S.S. Malakand

There was a loud explosion heard all over Wallasey when the 7,649 ton Brocklebank freighter *SS Malakand* was blown up in No.2 Branch Husskinson Dock, Liverpool on 3 May 1941. She had a thousand tons of high explosives in holds 1, 2, 3 and 7 and was due to sail to the Middle East. At about 11.15pm a partly-inflated barrage balloon came in contact with forestay and landed on the hatch, causing the covers to set alight. Captain Howard Kinley and his crew successfully fought the blaze with pumps for 15 minutes but a stick of incendiaries which fell on her decks became too much for the crew and Firemen. It went out of control and the men took refuge in a large shed. The vessel blew up with her plates landing two and a half miles away. A couple were killed by a falling plate as they drove along the Dock Road in Liverpool. It took some 74 hours before the explosions finished, however there were only four deaths.

During May 1941 1,453 people lost their lives through enemy action in Liverpool and in addition there were 1,065 people who were seriously injured.

Royal Daffodil

Just after 10pm on 7 May, during the May Blitz 1941, the ferryboat *Royal Daffodil II,* which had been built at Cammell Laird in 1934, received a direct hit and sank whilst moored at the Seacombe stage (*see photograph*). Either the bomb exploded on impact or went right through the ship and exploded in the mud beneath. The outcome was the ferryboat had a large hole near her starboard engine. There were 12 men below deck as the water gushed in. An Engineer was on the companion ladder at the time and was blown up and landed on the deck without injury but lost his false teeth! Some 13 months later she was brought to the surface covered with marine growth, mud and silt, her funnel and mast had been removed. She was refloated and repaired, returning to service in June 1943 and was later renamed *St Hilary* as a new boat was to have the name of *Royal Daffodil*. She and her sister ship, *Royal Iris,* had been used for ferrying the soldiers from the troop ships in the Mersey.

The *Marlowe* ferryboat was also damaged by a bomb as she was berthed at the Liverpool Landing Stage. Flying shrapnel struck Mate Frank Welch, causing injury.

The first of the May raids lasted for about two and a half hours and the next night for almost four hours and third night, from 11.00pm to 3.30am. On the fourth night, the raids did not start until well turned midnight until 4am and similar periods on the fifth, sixth and seventh nights.

The *Winter Gardens Theatre* was to suffer when a bomb fell on the old dressing rooms and Gorse Hill Reservoir was also damaged. A decoy 'Liverpool' was built on the mouth of the River Dee. It had some success as Major Victor Von Lossberg, a commander of a German pathfinder unit, could do nothing as the following Heinkels started to bomb the decoy site on 3 May 1941.

Wallasey escaped with having only three people killed and 19 seriously injured during May 1940 with 7,500 people being evacuated.

On a raid that took place on 1 June 1941 eight High Explosive Bombs fell in the area of St George's Park. An Air-Raid Warden named WJ Smythe was killed and others injured. The petrol pumps at Applerley's Garage in Rowson Street were damaged and caught fire but by the time the NFS arrived it had been successfully extinguished.

There was an air-raid on 25 June 1941 when houses were hit in the Dalmorton Road area and other roads in the town. It was not until November that the enemy dropped further bombs on the town with the Broadway Avenue district suffering damage. This was to be the last raid on Wallasey with the last bomb falling on Merseyside 10 January 1942.

In August 1941 all the Fire Services in the United Kingdom were nationalised and became known as the NFS (National Fire Service) in order to combat enemy action. The Firemen wore a large badge on the left side their tunics, replacing a similar one. Beneath was the name of the town. They wore a flat peaked-cap and their tunic had six metal buttons on either side. The wide belt had a leather holster for the axe. When fighting fires they wore an Army-type tin hat with the letters AFS on, later changed to NFS. The Discipline Code of Service was introduced.

Harold Jones, who was a ship broker, was a part-time Fireman in the NFS. He married his sweetheart, Lorna Smart, on 21 August 1941. He dressed in his best Sunday suit and his bride wore a nice two-piece outfit and matching hat. A dozen Firemen or so in uniform attended the wedding and the couple were taken to the reception on the back of a small lorry that was used as a fire-fighting vehicle with Pump Trailer in tow! The bride and groom had to climb up a ladder to get on and they stood among the stirrup pumps, buckets ladders and hoses as the crowd gave a cheer.

Mr William Nicholson was appointed Divisional Commander in charge of the Wirral Division, comprising of Bebington, Birkenhead and Wallasey.

The New Year Party, given by the Wallasey AFS, had been attended by 60 children.

Mr RW Giles who had a public house in Poulton, was also a wartime Fireman along with Max Halliwell, Cecil Kesterton, John Trott, Tom West, and many, many more. The well-known Wallasey Sunday School teacher and local Lay preacher, George Roche also joined the NFS George was well known as a magician and would give shows to various groups and clubs in the town. Years later he became the Part Time Secretary of the local YMCA. After the war, his brother, Walter, became editor of the old *Wallasey Chronicle.*

Bill Rivers was born at Hanley, near Stoke-on-Trent in 1911, the family moved to Wallasey and lived in Grange Avenue. After leaving St James's School, New Brighton he took a temporary job in Liverpool then in 1925 he joined the Wallasey Printers at ten shillings a week. He started work as a messenger boy with the *Wallasey News* whose office was in the same building as the *Five Bars Hotel*. Bill rose to advertising manager of the paper and eventually a director in 1962. He had joined the Fire Service as a part-time Fireman, later becoming full-time.

A Sub-Station was set up at Windsor's Garage, Harrison Drive with Trailer Pumps (The back of Windsor's garage received a direct hit demolishing the rear wall of the building); there was one at Spiller's Mills; a garage in Albion Street, New Brighton; a private garage in North Drive was used to house a Trailer Pump; another small Sub-Station was at the top of Leasowe Road by the Weigh Bridge stone building and the service garage in Rullerton Road housed one Fire Engine. The men were called out one evening to attend a fire in a field near Breck Road. One poor Fireman was unfortunate enough to fall into a cesspit. He was hauled out and his colleagues made him ride on the back of the Fire Engine on account the pong! Back at the Sub-Station he stripped off and stood naked while Fireman Syd Pope hosed him down in the Station Yard!

There was also a Fire Guard Depot at the old Liscard High School for Boys at the top of Hale Road. Douglas Cooper from Marlborough Road was one of the men there and a relative of his, Frank James Cooper, had served a number of years in the Acton Fire Brigade and received a Long Service Medal from the National

NFS on Parade at the Mayor's Sunday & Civil defence Day 15 November 1942

Fire Brigades' Association.

The old tunnels, that were once used by smugglers, under the New Palace, New Brighton were used as an air-raid shelter for a period. Then in March 1942 it became a war factory where 250 men and women worked on munitions. This small factory was able to produce as many as 250,000 machine-gun bullets casings, 25,000 25mm. shell casings and 1,400 switches for aircraft radios a week. They also made radar chassis. I remember a lady, Mrs Brenda Clark, who worked there. I think she was on a machine that made small steel curtain runners that were used for blackout curtains in our bombers. Her husband, Eric, was a full-time Civil Defence worker based at a First Aid Post in Sandrock Road. Another war factory was in Grosvenor Road, New Brighton where they made parts for submarines. This building was to suffer from bombing.

The enemy planes that attacked Merseyside were the four-seater Dornier Do 17Z - a two-engined high wing monoplane capable of 265mph known as the 'Flying Pencil' that had a maximum speed of 265mph and a bomb load of 2,205lbs.

The five-seater Heinkel HE 111 two-engined bomber with a crew of five. Top speed of 255mph and capable of carrying a bomb load of some 4,410lbs. and had a range of 2,640 miles.

The two-engined five-seater Dive Bomber Junkers JU 88 was capable of reaching 286mph and had a range of 1,553 miles with a bomb load of 5,510lbs. Some could carry as much as 6,614lbs.

The planes could reach an operational height of over 25,000ft. and their engines had been altered so as to distort the British sound locators. The planes were equipped with machine guns.

The four-engined Focke-Wuf was used for marine reconnaissance. The planes of the Luftwaffe coming to bomb Merseyside, took off from Luftflotte 2 and 3 Airfields in France, Belgium, Holland and North Germany. They flew over Cornwall and came in from the Irish Sea.

The British fighter planes were the famous Spitfire and Hawker Hurricanes. The former were easily manoeuvrable coupled with speed and machine guns. Later, came the twin-engined Bristol Beaufighter.

A number of dog-fights were witnessed over Merseyside, often resulting in enemy planes being shot down.

The 4.5 inch AA guns were able to fire a 56lb. shell eight miles into the sky in 50 seconds. There were also mobile Bofors and Lewis machine guns. It is recorded that the AA guns had brought down three or four enemy planes and four had been damaged. The fighters claimed four bombers. The AA guns had fired something in the region of 5,500 shells into the air. One civilian was killed by an AA shell that exploded on the ground.

The 'Hopper' AA guns at Green Lane in Leasowe could fire 80lb. shells. The Home Guard 'D' Company at Stoneycroft in Penkett Road relieved the regulars at the gun-site.

Rocket Batteries

A small number of Rocket 'Z' Batteries were established in the country which were known as un-rotated projectiles. One such battery was established here in Wallasey in 1941, sited on the golf links in Warren Park. Another in Sefton Park in Liverpool. 20 projectors were capable of firing 4,000 rockets into the sky simultaneously. The rockets were of 3in. calibre, six feet long and operated by soldiers of the Royal Artillery until 1942 when the 103rd Cheshire Home Guard took over. Being installed June 1944 six large Mark 20 barrel projectors were never used in anger and were removed in December 1944.

The bombs that fell on Merseyside were the High Explosive type and Land or Parachute Mines. The latter were usually the cylinder type and could be 12ft. long and two feet, two inches wide and constructed of aluminium. The parachutes, which were made of green silk, measured 15 feet when opened.

The 'G' Mines were dropped without the aid of parachutes.

There were sea mines that were dropped in the river.

The Incendiary Bombs, which were dropped in clusters, caused thousands of fires in the country. Some of these contained an explosive charge and scattered molten magnesium and steel splinters over a considerable distance. There was also the C300 Incendiary Bomb. Other types of bombs included:- the small 1kg. which had a cylindrical body being filled with therite and had a tail. Some of these had a bursting charge; the 50kg. which measured 3 foot six inches without vane; the semi-armour piercing one that was 3 foot three inches in length without vane; the 100kg. four foot, three inches; the longer 250 kg. was known as an 'Oil Bomb' on account of being filled with oil and a change of high explosive; the 500 kg. which was six feet ten and a half inches in length; the slightly smaller SAP type known as Esau'; the 1000kg. was just over nine feet long without vane and was known as 'Herman' . The 'Fritz' was a 1400 kg. SAP bomb that was 6 feet, three inches long without vane. The biggest was the 'Satan' general purpose bomb of 1800kg and was almost nine feet in length.

The bombs were fitted with percussion fuses that were intended to explode on impact. A 500lb. could create a blast speed of 3,000mph with a radius of 30 feet.

There was an incident when three US bombers that flew up the Mersey, having lost their way. The AA guns opened fire, but thankfully they were not hit and the planes climbed high to get out of range and headed off over the Irish Sea.

There was a suspect unexploded bomb scare when a house received a direct hit in Vicarage Grove. I think the German Prisoners of War came to dig but no bomb was found.

The old part of Earlston Library had also suffered during the air-raids, causing damage to east wing.

The Wallasey 'Z' or Rocket Battery was situated on a nine acre site below and to the south-west of Warren Drive

The Austin K2 Auxiliary Towing Vehicle was a reliable vehicle which were ordered by the Home Office in the early part of the Second World War. They were built on a two ton Austin chassis and were able to carry a crew of six on bench-type seats inside. The hoses and equipment were stored underneath and they pulled a pump and had a ladder of 30 feet which was carried on the roof. These were built to replace the converted taxis, vans and other motor vehicles that were rounded up to fight the fires. During the war period 9,000 were built. A version of the Austin K was adapted (the K4) with a Merryweather Turn-Table hand-operated ladder unit. Ford also produced ATVs which were heavier and stronger that their Austin counterpart.

Prior to the war Fire Brigades often purchased German Turn-Table Ladders.

Air Raid Sirens were first sounded in earnest on 17 November 1939 when a lone German Heinkel Reconnaissance plane was seen high in the sky over Wirral. The AA guns opened fire and puffs of smoke was seen in the sky but they were unable to hit the plane it got away.

Barrage Balloons were seen all over the town, being usually stationed in parks. Littlewood's Pool people actually produced 20,000 of these balloons in addition to shells, parachutes, pontoons etc.

On 10 January 1942 there were 1,500 spectators who watched New Brighton FC played Bury in the League War Cup at Gigg Lane where they lost by ten goals to five. Five of Bury's goals were scored by Urmston who was a Wallasey Policeman attached to the NFS at Wallasey.

When Lieut. Colonel JTC Moore-Brabazon was created a Baron and entered the House of Lords in 1942 it caused a bi-election in Wallasey. The Fire Brigade brought out an Escape and placed it in the recess opposite the Central Fire Station in Liscard Village. As the votes were counted they were displayed on the Escape so the public could see the number of votes cast for the each of the candidates.

By now the population of Wallasey had fallen from 100,000 odd to less than 40,000 as the many residents had gone to live in places that were safe from air-raids and this may have effected the result. Albeit, Mr George L Reakes, JP, who stood as an independent, was returned with a 6,012 majority. This was a surprise result as Wallasey was considered as a safe Tory seat. Mr Reakes had beaten another local Conservative Councillor, Mr John Pennington and Major LH Cripps, brother of Sir Stafford Cripps, and the Labour candidate.

Among the first men to answer the call for men to join the NFS was Henry (Harry) David Driscoll, an electrician who lived in Park Street. He became Section Leader, never failed to respond when duty called, his courage and self sacrifice set a model example to the rest of the men. He had been employed by the Wallasey Corporation before joining Messrs. Campbell and Isherwood of Liverpool. He died on 28 November 1942 aged 39. Six comrades of the NFS acted as bearers at the funeral at Rake Lane Cemetery when a large number of NFS men were present, headed by Chief Fire Inspector William Nicholson.

Enemy planes shot down

At 4pm on 8 October 1940 a Junkers approached from over the Irish Sea and flew up the Mersey, heading for Ellesmere Port. Three Hurricanes of the Czechoslovak 321 Squadron took off from Speke and crowds saw them attack an enemy bomber. Flt. Lt. DE Gilham, Pilot Officer A Vasatko and Sgt. J Stenik were the crews. The battle lasted eleven minutes. One of the Czech pilots, Sgt. Hanzicek, was killed when he baled out too low and his fighter crashed into the Mersey. The Junkers came down in a field in Bromborough with engines on fire. As it bumped along, two 500lb. bombs fell out. Smoke was pouring out of the port engine. Two of the crew pulled themselves out and ran behind the plane. Gateman Harry Gill was first on the scene (Mr Gill was later to become Mayor of Bebington). The two Germans were well-built men and he saw them bending over a third who was lying on the ground. Without a care, Harry hurried across and seized them by their epaulettes and demanded their guns. They handed them over. Being in the uniform of a Port Sunlight Gateman, they may have thought that he was a sort of Policeman. Two others arrived, a Mr Thompson and Mr Reid. Mr Thompson took charge of the two Luftwaffe men. One was 19 years old and had already made five raids over Merseyside. They were marched off to the Gatehouse where they were held in custody until the Military arrived. The member of the crew that was on the ground had suffered a broken thigh bone and was in pain. Harry and Mr Reid looked around and found a shunter's pole and bound his leg to it as a temporary splint.

The pilot of the plane had been killed by machine gun fire and had fallen forward over the controls. Close at hand was a detailed map of Merseyside with the storage tanks at Port Sunlight and Bromborough Dock clearly marked as targets. The crew had inflated a rubber dinghy as the pilot had hoped to bring his plane down in the river.

The RAF officials were very interested in the bombsight on the plane which they had not seen before. This was removed and was taken to the Gatehouse to be collected later.

Another of the Dorniers was piloted by Herr Gunther and after bombing Gladstone Dock was hit over New Brighton by the AA guns and the plane crashed in the River Dee where the crew swam ashore and gave themselves up to a Policeman.

Feldwebel Guenther Unger was pilot of a Junkers 88. He approached the Mersey at 10,000 feet to attack the shipping. Observer Feldwebel 'Ast' Meier was operating the Lotfe bombsight. They released four 550lb. and ten 110lb. bombs as the pilot noticed flames behind the starboard engine. He knew he would not be able to make home so he ordered his crew to bale out and Unger headed out to crash in the sea so that there would be nothing for the British to find. The plane was flying well and he considered whether he should try to get home in it but the blaze got worst. He parachuted out of the stricken plane. All the crew landed safely, save Unger. He was in the water and although it was shallow, it took him over an hour to wade to the Wallasey sands where he was confronted by a member of the Home Guard and gave himself up.

Hardy Voght was a Flight Engineer who flew on 45 bombing raids including Merseyside until he was shot down over Hertfordshire in April 1941 and became a prisoner of war.

In 1991, he returned to Wallasey to see the remains of the engine of his plane that is kept in the Military Aviation Museum at Perch Rock Battery at New Brighton.

******

Casualties

Fireman Ernest Richings, aged 30, of 55 Vyner Road, was killed on 12 March 1941 in Poulton Road.

Fireman Thomas Henry Roberts, aged 33 of 56 Byerley Street was injured on 13 March 1941, when a land mine fell on Lancaster Avenue and died later that day in the Cottage Hospital.

First Aid Post Ambulance driver Noel Richard Day, aged 40, who lived at 5 Lindeth Avenue, was killed by enemy action on 13 March 1941 at Central Park Recreation Ground.

Fireman William Rogerson, aged 37 from Longridge, Preston, was killed on 18 March 1941 at the East Float Docks while on duty.

Albert Charles James was a young man of 33 years who served

NFS taking part in the Victory Parade in front of
the Town Hall 19 May 1945

both in the Fire Brigade and the ARP. He lost his life on 22 September 1940 when his home was bombed at 30 Briardale Road. Fireman Percy Dearing, aged 27, who lived at 27 The Grove, lost his life when the Electric Works in Limekiln Lane was bombed on 20 December 1940.

Another Fireman to lose his life as a result of the bombing in Wallasey was that of George Harrison of 23 Ivor Road who died at the Cottage Hospital on 13 March 1941. He was 39 years old.

There had been 43 raids over Wallasey with 509 alerts and 658 High Explosive Bombs had fallen on the borough, including 17 Parachute Mines. As many as 1,150 houses had been demolished and a further 17,000 houses were damaged.

Several churches were damaged by the bombing including the redbrick Roman Catholic on the corner of Hope Street and Rowson Street, which was completely wrecked, as was the Methodist Church in Poulton Road. Rowson Street Methodist and St Luke's Church were also hit, the latter suffered much damage to the roof. The Salvation Army Hall in Poulton was slightly damaged as was St John's Church and Hebron Hall suffered a fire. The new St Peter and St Paul's Church in Atherton Street was guarded by Father Mullins but was eventually persuaded to retreat to the shelter under the Hotel Victoria for his own safety.

Merseyside had suffered 68 raids, 3,966 people had been killed and 3,812 seriously injured.

During the war (in 1943) we see the following living in Manor Road:-

No.4 Allan Jackson, Police Fireman
No.6 Thomas Garner, NFS worker
No.14 Richard Webster, Fireman
No.18 Miss Isobel McCamley, midwife
No.20 Mrs Winstanley
No.3 PC John Henry Williams
No.4 Samuel G Pink, Fireman
No.7 Leonard A Barnes, Fireman
No.9 Robert Jones, Police Fireman
No.21 PC Joseph William Barke
No.23 PC Ivan Maddocks (went into the Fire Brigade)

No.27 Harold Winstanley, painter
No.29 Herbert Winstanley, Police Fireman
(The first house in Manor Road was said to be haunted.)
In Daventree Road:-
No.9 PC Jonathan Thorley
No.23 PC Peter Roberts
In Egerton Grove:
12 Joe Riley, Fireman

Jack Heulett who lived in Caldy Road was the Police Storekeeper. He also trained the police in Self Defence and had been a professional boxer in his younger days. He once told me that he had fought Ernie Roderick, the British Welter Weight Champion. After the war, many people will recall him as a second at the New Brighton Tower wrestling with Wryton Promotions. He was still keen on boxing and passed on some of his skills to the lads at the local YMCA in Manor Road.

In the summer of 1944 the band of the National Fire Service played for the Stand Down March of the Home Guard in Central Park where the salute was taken by the Mayor of Wallasey, Alderman John Pennington. With him were Officers of the Allied Forces.

The Home Office agreed in 1944 that the Wartime discipline arrangements were a suitable basic for Peacetime service. The Discipline Code of the NFS remained until the break-up of the Service.

The Fireman's pay was in line with that of a Policeman and the Fire Brigade Pensions were similar to that of the Police.

After the war, a monument was erected in the far end of Rake Lane Cemetery commemorating the civilians that had lost their lives through enemy action. The inscription reads:-

This memorial is erected to honour the 334 noncombatant
residents of Wallasey of whom 51 rest here who lost
their lives by air attack from the enemy
during the Second World War, 1939-1945.

A further Memorial Plaque was dedicated at the Town Hall on 16

February 2001 to the Citizens of Wallasey who lost their lives in the Second World War. The Memorial Service was conducted by Rev Bruce Harry and the Plaque was unveiled by the Mayor of Wirral, Councillor Kate Wood.

Twelve Wardens died as a result of the air-raids during the period 1940-41.
Here are the number of civilian causalities:

August	1940	9 killed	10 seriously injured.
September	1940	4 killed	2 seriously injured.
October	1940	3 killed	3 seriously injured.
November	1940	3 killed	3 seriously injured.
December	1940	119 killed	91 seriously injured.
January,	1941	2 killed	3 seriously injured.
February	1941	2 killed	3 seriously injured
March	1941	189 killed	158 seriously injured.
May	1941	3 killed	19 seriously injured.

In addition to those who were killed, 275 were seriously injured in the raids on the town and there were over 600 people that were slightly injured. It was in May 1941, that 1,453 people lost their lives through enemy action in Liverpool and in addition there were 1,065 people who were seriously injured.

1945

After the war, the Wallasey Fire Brigade had a collection of appliances. There were four Fire Engines and three Trailer Pumps which were manned by a full-time staff of 58 Firemen.

******

Mr. Joseph Holt

Mr Joseph Holt, who came from Blackburn, was originally a millwright, used to handling ropes and operating machinery which led him to being a good Fireman. He started his career in the Fire Service by joining the Leeds City Police Fire Brigade in 1924 then was the successful applicant for the vacancy of Sergeant at Wallasey in April 1929. He became the youngest Sergeant in the country and Third Officer of the Wallasey Police Fire Brigade in May 1929. He brought his uniform and boots along for which the Council had to compensate Leeds City Police for £7.19s.6d. He was appointed Inspector in 1940, became Deputy Chief Fire Officer in 1941, then a Column Officer and was promoted to Divisional Commander to succeed Mr Nicholson.
Mr Holt became Chief Fire Officer of the Wallasey Fire Brigade in 1948.

Wallasey Fire Chief Joseph Holt leads a parade of Firemen past St George's School, Wallasey Village

Ted Phillips

Ted Phillips joined the NFS in 1947 at Hatton Garden, having been demobbed from the army, serving in the 1st and 8th Armies in North Africa and Italy. He was transferred to the Wallasey Fire Brigade in 1948 and became known as 'Captain' as for some ten years he was the grand owner of a boat moored on the Shropshire Canal.
His son John suffered from polio and was in a plaster-cast for two years. Whilst he was in hospital, Frank Uriel made him a fort and his sister a doll's house complete with lights and garage.
Ted bought an ex-Fire Brigade motorcycle and sidecar for £20 and ex-colleague, Jack Sheen, who was good at woodwork, made a hood and support so that Ted could take his son out for a ride.
Ted was the member of the crew that went out on a special call-out on New Brighton foreshore at Harrison Drive involving the rescue of a pony and rider who were stuck on the rocks and in danger from the incoming tide. The rider was soon rescued but the pony was still trapped. Eventually the animal was brought to the sea wall and with Ted holding onto the boots of one of his colleagues, although the pony was lassoed in real John Wayne style, it remained in the water. However, a huge wave washed the animal right over the railings and was saved.
Ted and the rest of the team (Jack Wright, David Bagley, Jeffrey Toland, Kevin Foxley and Gordon Beck) received commendations from the Chief Fire Officer and the RSPCA.
Ted retired in 1970 on medical grounds and received a lump sum of £1,700 and a pension of £8 a week.
He purchased the old Fire Station clock and had it repaired and proudly has it on his wall at home along with the old brass bell which he rescued from the old Fire Engine known as 'Leaping Lena', before it was taken away for scrap.

Flour Mills

Although the Dock Road Mills were in Wallasey, all fire and accident calls were put through to Birkenhead and then to Wallasey. When there was a fire alarm at Rank's or Home Pride Mills the Birkenhead Fire Brigade would turn out and they would notify the Wallasey Fire Brigade. Sometimes the bridges would be up which would delay the Birkenhead Brigade. Which ever Brigade arrived first dealt with the fire and the other Brigade would help if required or return to their station.
The Birkenhead Brigade had to be invited in when there was a big fire as they could not come in on their own initiative.
The problem with a fire at a flour mill was the explosions caused by flour dust. To help to combat this small tissue bags filled with stone dust were placed by the conveyer belts. When the first explosion occurred, the bags would burst and spread the stone dust into the air which would kill off the explosive mixture. Explosions at flour mills were capable of blowing the end gable wall out.
Mr. Holt would turn a blind eye to those Firemen who would try to get a few hours' sleep whilst on watch, but he insisted that there be a full crew should there be a Call-Out. The Firemen would sleep half-dressed and all they had to do was to pull their trousers and boots. Their tunics were packed on the Engine and they could dress as they raced along. The tunic would become very heavy when it got wet and the smell of the smoke would linger for days When they were discarded, they could be cut and made into hearth rugs.
Rank consisted of Chief Fire Officer, Column Officer (later called Sub. Officer), Company Officer/ Station Officer, Section Leader, Leading Firemen and Firemen. There was also Sub Officers. The Section Leader was in charge of a Watch. Later came Assistant Divisional Officers, Divisional Officers and Chief Divisional Officers.

Firemen tackling a flour mill fire

The Brigade covered an area of some 15 square miles with a population of 106,000. The Brigade cost £25,000 a year to operate. The telephone number was Wallasey 2222-3 or Wallasey 3486 and was later changed to 638 2134 which included the Ambulance service.

Water hydrants were used by the Brigade for the supply of water and if there was a faulty one the Firemen moved to the next available one. Regular tests were carried out to see that they were kept in working order.

A Fireman was not allowed to be on the Turn-Table ladder when it rose to its full height as he could be severely burned from the heat of the flames due to the heat-band around a large fire. The practice was to send up the ladder, which was of bright metal, and if it became darkened, they would know that it was too dangerous from that position.

The Wallasey Fire Brigade asked the Home Office to establish a Fire Station in Moreton to improve call-out times there but they stated that Birkenhead Fire Brigade's application for a Fire Station at Upton was preferred, as Moreton was in easy reach of there.

The Fire Brigade Regional Training School was housed at St Joseph's Longsight in Manchester which was under the command of Divisional Officer Graham Canham.

The Leyland Pump Escapes were capable of supplying 1,000 gallons of water a minute by either using the street hydrants or taking water by suction from rivers, lakes or docks. The trouble with the British hydrants was that they were underground unlike the American ones which were above. In winter the cover could be covered in snow or frozen.

The men often had trouble getting their tunics on whilst holding onto the rail as the engine was travelling around bends at speed on the way to the fire.

Wallasey Road by the *Boot Inn* was always a difficult bend to negotiate and on one occasion Billy Higham was thrown off the Engine there and landed outside the Boot Inn's front door – surely there must have been an easier way to call in for a pint! The driver did not have time to dress until they reached the fire.

The Fireman's leather fire boots were later replaced with rubber ones but the soles and toe caps were not as strong as the leather boots and sharp objects such as broken glass or protruding nails, could go right through the rubber boots and injure the Fireman. Firemen also found them to be slippy on wet surfaces. They were later replaced with a rubber boot that had three soles and a metal toe-capbut the rubber boots became hot while fighting a fire.

Human Christmas Tree

Another amusing incident at the Central Fire Station was when the men were carrying out an exercise with the fully-extended 60ft. Turntable Ladder. The Firemen were on the fully extended ladder when Sam Pemberton called out:

"OK boys, make up."

With a lapse of concentration, the ladder was unclipped and somehow all the men were taken by surprise and were left hanging on the back like Christmas decorations on a Christmas tree! Luckily, all ended well.

On another occasion, the Brigade went to a fire in Hope Street, New Brighton with Harold Cash in charge. The Engine hit a bump in the road causing the wood of the Escape to snap. When they got back to the Station the men had trouble getting it off the Engine.

Day to Day

But of pleasures there are many and of worries there are none;
And of the culminating pleasure
That we treasure beyond measure
Is the gratifying feeling that our duty has been done!
WS Gilbert

With the older Pumps (Engines), the crew had to stand on the side of the vehicle and were exposed to the cold wind as the Engine rushed to the fire. When the men were fighting a fire, the force of the water from the hoses needed two to four men to hold them.

Suction hoses were used at a fire at the docks. These could be dropped into the dock and water pumped out.

For smaller fires the defuse jets could be opened up as a wide spray, preventing the heat from reaching the Fireman and acting as a water curtain, or closed down to make a jet. Fires could be driven the way the Firemen wished it to go. The main part of the fire would be attacked and smaller outbreaks could be ignored.

Like today, the Fire Service had emergency cover. When the Wallasey Brigade was out on a fire, Engines from Birkenhead, Bebington, West Kirby, Heswall or Liverpool could be called on if necessary. If all the Engines from these Stations were used they would then call on Chester or Cheshire Brigades. A five-pump fire could result in moving as many as 25 fire Engines for cover. The practice is somewhat different today. Years ago, Firemen stayed on a fire to the end whereas now they do four hours and come off. If there was a thick fall of snow the Appliances would be fitted with tyre chains to get a grip.

Not since the Great Fire of London has there been a charge for calling out the Brigade for a fire, but for Special Services, such as dealing with a fallen TV aerial, a charge can be made.

There was a case when a 'Do-it-Yourselfer' went up on his roof, lost his nerve and had to call the Brigade out to get him down. A similar thing happened to a contractor/plumber who had been working on a roof on his own.

Some years ago a lady in Liscard got her finger stuck in the outlet of a copper washing boiler and the Brigade came to her rescue.

If a child got its head stuck between railings, the Firemen would use margarine or grease to release it.

In cases of a False Alarm with good intent, this is classed as a Fire Call and no charge is made.

There have been cases of people being locked out. This is known as a Lockout. When the Firemen arrive at the house, the first thing they have to do is to establish the fact that the person who made the call actually lives in the house. There have been cases of the Brigade getting into a house for a person who turned out to be a burglar! 'Lock Outs' can be chargeable.

Reviving a pet such as a cat or dog that had been rescued from a fire, a Fireman would remove his tunic and make it into a sort of oxygen tent. The animal would be placed inside and the oxygen would be pushed up the sleeve.

When dealing with a frightened horse during a fire, one of the men would take off his tunic and cover the horse's head with it in order to calm the animal.

Drill was an important part of the Fire Service. The men spent many hours going over various routines until the Station Officer was satisfied with their efficiency.

Fitness of the men was important and sport was encouraged with those on Watch encouraged to play volley ball in the Station Yard at the back of the Fire Station (this game is no longer played on account of accidents).

Tug Boat

Harry Cash and others were called to a Lamey tugboat that was taking in water while in dock. When the Brigade arrived an engineer was sitting on a valve and when he rose to his feet water poured in. It was faulty so he had covered it with some overalls and had been holding it in place until help arrived. The firemen soon had it fixed and all was well again!

Film Stars

When the Ealing Studio film crew came to make "The Magnet" in Wallasey, the director, Charles Frend came to the Wallasey Fire Brigade and asked for help. Three Firemen were chosen to play a small part in the film, namely Ted Jones, Johnny Ellison and Bill Forber.

A Liverpool Policeman was also asked to take part in a scene which involved the Wallasey Firemen.

Bill Forber, who had been a joiner working for Critchton's in Liverpool, got married and joined the Wallasey Fire Brigade on 3 December 1948. He served with the Brigade for a many years and had to leave due to ill health in March 1975. His son followed in his father's footsteps and became a Fire-Fighter and is at present stationed at West Kirby.

Union Matters

Ten minutes since I met a chap
Who bowed an easy salutation-
Thinks I, "This gentleman, mayhap,
Belongs to our Association.

WS Gilbert

When Harold Cash retired from the Fire Brigade, the men laid on a party for him. The sad part about it was that he had to give up the house he was living in and the Town Clerk had written to him asking to be out of the house within seven days.

The men became concerned with the consequences if they met with an accident and had to leave the Fire Service.

Fireman Charles Best, being the Union man, wrote a letter to the Town Clerk about the situation and he discovered there were no conditions drawn up concerning the Firemen's 'tied' houses and all he was told was "You don't think we would put you out of your home."

Mick Johnson, Charlie Graham and Ken Thompson spoke up for the Union and it was decided that Charlie Best and Taffy Redmoor would go to see the Town's Member of Parliament about the matter in hope that he could do something on their behalf. To make their point more effective, they decided to keep their children off school and get the mothers to take them up to Derby House, the Conservative Head Quarters in Rake Lane.

Some of the youngsters were well behaved but a number got bored waiting and started to play on the rockery.

Mr Ernest Marples arrived on his bicycle (he was known for cycling around London) and wondered what all the children were doing. He spoke to them and once he knew what it was all about, he listened to the Fireman's problem.

He explained the rights of farm workers living in cottages owned by the farmer and he, too, had workers that lived in houses that were part of his vineyard in Spain. He wrote to the Town Hall and a meeting was arranged with the Watch Committee. Meanwhile, Councillor Dan Kennedy and Councillor Walter Jones had been approached and a draft of suitable proposals with all their demands were given to the Councillors. An agreement was reached.

The Wallasey Fire Brigade became one of the most democratic and efficiently run Brigades in the country.

Charlie Best was born in West Derby, being one of three boys. He

A Leyland Cub, which was used in the film The Magnet, *outside Seacombe Congregational Church Hall, Liscard Road (which was used as a film studio). Lt. to Rt. Bill Hughes, Driver; Norman Newton; Billy Forber; Les Pugh and Ted Phillips standing Lt.*

Wallasey Firemen in action at a dock fire with the Leyland Cub in 1948

went away to sea at the tender age of 14 with the Alfred Holt (Blue Funnel) Line. At the outbreak of the Second World War, he was called up for the Army and sent to France with the BEF. He was captured at Dunkirk and became a Prisoner of War for five years with some of this time being spent in the mines. On being demobbed from the Army, he decided to join the NFS in April 1946 then he married a girl named Frances; they went on to have five children. He chose to serve with the Wallasey Fire Brigade and took a great interest in the welfare of the men, being the Union Representative. Chas wrote a short history of the Wallasey Fire Brigade for *The Phoenix*, the Fire Brigade magazine.

He retired from the Brigade in 1975 and still lives in Manor Road where he has a handmade model of a Fire Engine which was given to him by the men and is displayed in the fanlight above the front door.

Over the years the Union have fought for better working conditions.

Today, a Firemen cannot be dismissed from the Fire Service by the Chief Fire Officer but the case has to go to a higher level. He can, if the decision goes against him, appeal to the Home Secretary.

******

MV Matrona

Elder Dempster's *MV Aba* (built 1918 & rebuilt 1921) arrived at Birkenhead Docks in January 1947 and was laid up in Bidston Dock. Not long after, she was purchased by Bawtry SS Company of London and the vessel was renamed *Matrona*. Alterations were carried out and on 30 October 1947, the vessel capsized and sank on her side in the dock. The Brigade was called out but Birkenhead Brigade had received the call first and were first to arrive on the scene. Little could be done and there were no loss of life. Ian Fraser VC had a diving company and his men were instrumental in righting the ship. The funnel and masts were later removed and divers set about sealing the hull. While this was taking place, 3,500 tons of concrete was poured into a long trench. When all was completed, 14 winches were secured to the concrete and each had a nine inch steel cable attached to the hull and in June 1948, the winches went into action and slowly the vessel was righted. The operation had been completed in 20 minutes. It was discovered that the vessel was not worth restoring and it was eventually towed to Barrow-in-Furness where it was scrapped for pig iron. She had been the world's first diesel-propelled ocean-going passenger liner.

******

Return to Local Authority

When the Fire Service returned to the control of the Local Authority in 1948, it was without the Police link, who had also relinquished control of the Ambulance Service. This was brought about through Section 2 of the Fire Service Act 1947. Under the Act Brigades had to be responsible for the ambulance service.

The Firemen wore a small metal badge with 'County Borough of Wallasey' on a red enamel circle with the shield from the Town's Coat of Arms in the centre.

Chief Fire Officer Mr Joseph Holt had a Deputy Chief Fire Officer (ADO), two Station Officers, four Sub Station Officers, four Leading Firemen and 47 Firemen. The Brigade had 64 men in all ranks under his control. They wore a large solid black helmet and special waterproof leggings over their trousers. The Appliances for 1948 consisted of two Major Pumps which were able to deliver 500 gallons per minute; one Pump Escape Major, which as well as being a Life-Saving appliance, was also capable of delivering water at the same rate as the other two Major Pumps; the 60ft. Austin-Merryweather TLP (this Ex NFS Ladder could be also used as a Water Tower or Life-Saving appliance – later replaced with an AEC-Merryweather 100ft. TL/P in 1960). The term 'tower' refers to the Turntable Ladder when it is extended to the necessary height with a man at the top sending down a jet of water on to the roof of the burning building. The grey-painted Austin K4/Merryweather 60ft.Escape was produced for the NFS during the Second World War. Fifty were built at the Austin Motor Co. Ltd. Works at Longbridge, Birmingham. They had a 3.5 litre six-cylinder Austin petrol engine with four-speed gearbox and hydraulic brakes. The five ton vehicle had a manually-operated 60ft. three section Turntable ladder. A number had a front-mounted 350 gpm pump. There were three Trailer Pumps and a variety of pumps that were useful for fire fighting or Special Service Calls.

The average number of fires in the borough was 105 per annum. There were six Ambulances and one Ambulance saloon car which were controlled from the Central Fire Station. The service dealt with 3,854 cases in previous year (1947).

For the year 1948, there were 184 Fire Calls, 36 Special Service Calls, 15 Malicious Calls and 21 Non Malicious Calls - a total of 256. High risk areas were the Flour Mills on the Dock estate, also timber and oil storage installations.

The Ambulance Service had answered some 9,134 calls.

Cost of running the Brigade for the year was £25,000.

The Fire Brigade had radios fitted and used the same frequency as the police with the Call-sign CWF and BNF.

On the retirement in 1944 of the Divisional Commander, William Nicholson, he was succeeded by his former Deputy, Mr Joseph Holt. Four years later, Mr Holt became Chief Fire Officer of the Wallasey Fire Brigade with Harold Cash as Deputy.

Rank consisted of Fire Chief Officer, Column Officer (later called Sub- Officer), Company Officer/ Station Officer, Section Leader, Leading Firemen and Firemen. There were also Sub-Station Officers, four Leading Firemen and 47 Firemen. The Brigade had 64 men in all ranks under his control.

New Ambulances

When the Fire Brigade took delivery of the two new Daimler Ambulances, it was suggested that next day they would be brought to the Town Hall so that the Watch Committee could see them. Two drivers were chosen to take the newly designed vehicles to the Town Hall. However, one of the men said he knew all about the new type of engine and had driven them in the Army. He jumped into the Ambulance, started up the engine, put it in gear and next minute had driven right through the doors of the Divisional Training School buildings in Liscard Crescent, taking the crisscross plate glass windows with it. The new ambulance was damaged and was supposed to be going down to the Town Hall at 10 o'clock!

The Chief was informed what had happened and was very vexed and he and Walter Meacock went to see the damage to the new Ambulance. The mechanic from the workshop was called and he beat out the damage. Meanwhile, contact had been made with a supplier in Liverpool who had the right shade of green paint and it duly arrived. The damaged area was quickly resprayed and no one could tell the difference.

The two ambulances were now ready and arrived at the Town Hall at the appointed time; the demonstration went off without further incident.

Many years later, Walter was attending a funeral of a Fireman when a man came up to him and said to him, "Don't you remember me?" – it was the driver who had crashed the ambulance.

******

Robert Begg

Fireman Bobby Begg became a Column Officer and took great pride in his dress. He would go to Mr Zabludow, the Liscard tailor and get his uniform tailor-made. He also would purchase his own patent leather boots for Parades and use a rougher type for every day duty.

He first lived in Manor Road and later moved to Barnwell Avenue. He had been a Marine Engineer and knew a lot about shipping and was inclined not to mix with the men and one night gave a lecture on 'fire procedures on ships'. He erected a blackboard and easel and pointed out the various details with a stick. He went on to speak about the crew's quarters at the fo'c'sle and other things concerning the crew.

The seamen could appeal to the Captain, should they have a complaint. They would draw straws and the one with the shortest would be the man to see the Captain on behalf of the others. At this point, he stopped and said:

"You fellows are all in the Union."

Rubber Warehouse Fire

In 1949 there was a fire in the Latex Rubber Warehouse in Gladstone No.2 Branch Dock in Liverpool and Black smoke drifted over the city. Ships in the dock were quickly moved away from the scene and the Wallasey Fire Brigade was called to help. After the fire was put out they found that all the hoses were caked in moulted rubber. As the Firemen tried to recover the hoses, some fell into the River and floated across the Mersey, ending up wrapped around the supports of the New Brighton Pier. All the hoses were marked and they were able to identify which Brigade that they belonged to. Getting the solidified rubber off them was quite a problem so special 100ft. long troughs had to be constructed which were filled with a chemical to separate the rubber. Different crews had to take turns in going over to Liverpool to use the troughs where the quayside was covered with the baked rubber as well as the railway lines. Men worked for several days before it was all removed.

Dave Glyn Jones who joined the Wallasey Fire Service in 1949 (see below)

******

DG Jones

Dave Glynn Jones joined the Wallasey Fire Service in 1949. He was a blacksmith by trade with Jones and Williams and was brother-in-law of Walter Peach. During the Second World War he served in the Royal Marines.

Dave decided to study hard and passed several Fire Service examinations resulting in promotion. He received Long Service and Good Conduct medals in 1972 and retired from the Brigade as ADO at Birkenhead in 1980 at the age of 55 having completed 30 years service.

Fine Spirit

Mr GH Charters, MBE, HM Inspector of Fire Brigades carried out the 1949 Annual Inspection. "You have some fine lads here", he said as he inspected the Firemen.

"There's a fine spirit among the men. Even those who were off duty turned in for the Parade", answered Mr Holt.

1950s

The Wallasey Fire Brigade were called out five times on Friday 27 January 1950. First at 8.15am to a chimney fire in Woodstock Road; at 9.15am they were called to a hearth fire in Gerard Road; at 11.29am to a closed-in hearth fire in Blackheath Road, Leasowe. Then at 12.40pm there was a False Alarm with Good Intent in Church Road. They also dealt with a chimney fire along the same road.

A new Daimler Ambulance was added at the cost of cost £2,000 and was taken down on Thursday 20 April 1950 at 5.30pm to the Town Hall for the Committee to inspect . It was hoped that a similar vehicle would be purchased for the sitting patients.

5,5000 patients were taken to hospital by the Ambulance in 1949.

The 1950 Annual Inspection was carried out by HM Inspector of Fire Brigades, Mr. GH Charters, MBE.

The fleet in the early 1950s consisted of two Ambulances, later increased to six, five being kept at the Divisional Training School in Liscard Crescent. One ambulance was kept at the Manor Road Station. Two were Leyland Automatic. There were three Ambulances: Major Pump, a Pump Escape and a PE Light. The latter had a pump at the front of the vehicle. There was also a Home Coventry Climber and the Brigade had a Rescue Platform. First out on a Call Out would be the Major Pump. The Major Pumps carried 500 to 1000 gallons of water (Fire Engines are classed by the output of the pump, being Major Pumps, Light Pumps and Heavy Pumps). Brigades were using the Siebe Gorman 'Proto' oxygen sets in the 1950s which had an hour's gas supply. Goggles, mouthpiece and a peg for the nose were all necessary.

The Police still had a connection with the Fire Brigade and it was not until 1951 that they became completely separate. The Firemen received 19/6 a week pay rise to £6.18s.6d with a maximum of £7.19s.6d and worked a 60 hour week with some larger Brigades operating an 80 hour week due to shortage of men. The Police received £7.13s.10d with a maximum of £9.14s.6d and worked a duty 48 hour week. The Chief Constable thought the discipline of the Wallasey Fire Brigade could have been better and he expressed his opinion.

The Fire Brigade Union was founded in 1918 but it was not until 1951 that it had any real effect. Unionism had started in 1906 but it was not until the First World War that numbers increased.

Some members of the Wallasey Fire Brigade were involved in the 'Spit and Polish' boycott. The Wallasey Fire Brigade Committee imposed fines of £1 and £2 according to the number of charges.

The Wallasey Fire Brigade decided to enter the 1951 Marine Park Regatta which was held on the Marine Lake, New Brighton where the 'A' Team won the Wade Harris Trophy. The crew members were D Jones, R Alexander and Jack Winstanley (Cox).

1951 saw a number of workmen trapped when a petrol drum ignited causing a hut in Edgehill Road, Moreton to burn. The alarm was raised and Brigades from Wallasey and Birkenhead raced to the scene. The Firemen managed to drag all the trapped men out through a window who were then taken to the Victoria Central Hospital and Birkenhead General Hospital.

A combination stove caught fire in a classroom at Clarendon High School in the same year. When the Brigade arrived they quickly brought the fire under control while the children were evacuated into the School Hall.

The 1951 Annual Inspection was carried out by Colonel GHR Halland, CIE, OBE, HM Inspector of Fire Brigades.

The Fire Brigade gave instruction to both the Boy Scouts and the Girl Guides to enable them to obtain their badges.

Firewomen

The first Firewoman in the Wallasey Fire Brigade, after the war period was, I believe, Marion Nolan. Among the other ladies that followed were:- Bernette Davies, who was on the switchboard joined the Fire Service at the age of eighteen and retired after 30 years' service; Joan Dyer; Diane Longworth, (whose father was the well-known Wallasey cycle dealer); and Hilary Porter. Special mention must be made of Francis Howard, who loyally served for many years in the AFS dating back to the dark days of the war. Romance blossomed and Joan Dyer married Fireman Gordon Beck and Marion Nolan Rose married Mr Uriel, the Fire Prevention Officer. Gordon had two brothers, Harry and Ronnie, who were also in Wallasey Fire Brigade. Harry had been transferred from the Liverpool Fire Brigade.

The Firewomen wore an attractive peaked cap and double-breasted tunic.

When the Fire Brigade became part of Merseyside, all the Firewomen went to work in Liverpool.

I understand that there were two civilian male workers that were also employed by the Brigade at one time.

Trick Call-Out

A favourite trick of youth gangs was to call out the Fire Brigade. They would gather a mass of leaves and paper, set fire to them in an entry and call the Fire Brigade. The men would turn out in full kit, but often or not they knew what the trouble was but that made no difference; it was still a Call-Out.

Jack Wright

Fireman John Wright became a Station Officer and Ambulance Officer when some of the ambulances were kept at Demesne Street. There were well over 20 Ambulance-men under his jurisdiction in 1952. Jack was one of the greatest characters at Wallasey. He was a very keen sportsman, particularly as a soccer player. He retired on Thursday 17 September 1981, having completed 30 years with the Fire Service.

To mark the occasion a special event was arranged at Cadbury's in Moreton. Two football matches were played; the first between the Control Room Girls v The Firemen of Yesteryear, which the girls won 6 goals to 3 and the second between the Officers and the Firemen which the Firemen won 3 goals to 2. In the evening a social was arranged at Cadbury's Social Club when Mr Buschenfeld presented Jack with an axe-mounted plaque and other gifts. He is connected with the cricket and football teams and encourages the Duke of Edinburgh Award training. He is also an active member of St Andrew's Church, New Brighton where he is the Welcoming Steward. His daughter, Mrs Ruth Daniels, is a Local Preacher.

Gales

The gales were so fierce in December 1952 that they brought down a 40ft. chimney at the Manx Cleaners in Gosvenor Drive, New Brighton. The Fire Brigade under the direction of Chief Fire Officer, Mr Joseph Holt, was called out. Mrs Edna Barrow was released by sawing through a heavy bearer and she was taken to the Victoria Hospital. Two other people were also injured by the fall of debris.

Empress Boat

The Wallasey Fire Brigade was called out to help when the 20,325 ton Canadian Pacific Railway luxury liner, *Empress of Canada* (originally the *Duchess of Richmond*) that caught fire in her berth in Gladstone Dock, Liverpool on Sunday 25 January 1953. They had just completed her annual overhaul. 200 men fought the fire which had broken out at about 3.45pm. It was a case of men being needed more than pumps. Fire Engines and crews were called in from all over the area. Water was pumped from the docks. After fighting the fire for six hours, all the men had to be called off at 10pm as the stricken liner listed over. The Firemen then fought from the roof of the shed and others from within. Finally, Sir Rex Hodges, the then manager of the Mersey Docks and Harbour Board announced that they would let it burn itself out. With the amount of water that had been pumped into the ship it caused it to heel over to port and the funnels and masts snapped and the liner keeled over shortly before 1.30am. The Fire Tender vessel *Vigilant* had been in attendance. A large Fire-Boat as such is equal to 25 very powerful pumps, and on account of drawing water from the dock itself, they never run out of water.

The ship was not raised until 6 March 1954 when a similar operation was carried out to the raising of the *Matrona* in the Bidston Dock. A-frames were welded to the starboard side of the

The Empress of Canada *had keeled over in Gladstone Dock following a fire on board*

hull then cables were attached which ran across the dock basin and through the sheds to the powerful steam winches that had been set into the road beyond. My brother Ron Smith, was there as a press photographer, took impressive photographs as the steam from the hoppers that were moored at the dock side turned the winches and slowly the hulk rose to a upright position (*see photo*). In September 1954 Dutch tugs took her to the breaker's yard in Spetia in Italy.

Dennis Pump

The Brigade took delivery of a Dennis F12 Pump Escape in 1953 (registration No. BHF 556) which was capable of delivering some 400gpm and had a Rolls Royce engine. This Appliance had the 150 wheelbase of the F7 and mechanically identical to that version with a 900gpm No.3 Dennis Pump which was placed amidships but had a raised frontal appearance. The F7 of 1949 also had a petrol engine and the Rolls Royce B80 MKX, which could reach the speed of 60mph in 45 seconds, was followed by a smaller pump, a Dennis F-8 Pump (CHF 606) which handled 200gpm.

This appliance also had a Rolls Royce B60 petrol engine with an output of 175 BPH. It had a five-speed gearbox, a Dennis No.2 Water Pump which delivered 500 GPM at 100 psi and a 200 gallon first aid water tank. Later models carried 250 gallons and had a 10ft. x 6ft. x 6ft. wheelbase. These appliances were highly

successful throughout the country.

The F12 Appliance was put through a speed test along Leasowe Road with Police escort and reached the speed of 80mph.

The old records proved that the old Horse-Drawn Fire Brigade could get down to *Seacombe Ferry Hotel* quicker than this new appliance which included getting the horses from the stable or paddock on the other side of the road. The men found this fact hard to believe.

In those days, a Constable, on hearing the bell of the Fire Engine being rung, would step into the road and take control of the traffic to allow a clear road for the Fire Engine. Later on, the Constable took no notice. One must remember there was much less traffic in those days and few traffic lights etc.

The Fire Engines then carried about 10 or 12 grease guns at the rear for lubrication. This enabled the men to grease right through to the front while the Engine was in use. These guns worked by screwing them from the back end.

The crew of an Engine was about five or six men with the Leading Fireman being a man who had received extra training and could take responsibly for being in charge of a Pump. A Company Officer could be in charge of five Pumps and a larger number for a Station Officer. The Column Officer had similar responsibilities.

After the Chief Fire Officer came his Deputy, then the Column Officer (Station Officer was later), followed by the Company Officer. There were Section Leaders, Leading Fireman and the Firemen.

The Fire Brigade attended to many minor fires in the town including that one at Clarendon High School in 1954.

The Second New Brighton Tower Fire

There had been a fire at the New Brighton Tower in 1915, but was it was not until forty years later that a serious fire threatened the huge building. This happened on Thursday evening 20 January 1955. Fire had broken out in the cafe on the third floor and only a well separated it from the large ballroom. Prompt action by the Ballroom Manager, Mr. Cyril Isherwood and the Watchman, saved the Ballroom. The Manager walked out of his office and across the Ballroom floor when he saw a flicker of light in the cafe. At first, he thought it was the light from the geyser. He went to investigate and raised the alarm at 7.25pm then together with the watchman, John Williams, they fought the flames using a mobile extinguisher until the Brigade arrived. The Wallasey Fire Brigade

A group of Firemen posing in front of the Turn-Table Ladder

Dennis F24 pump with yellow livery 1958

Mr. Holt

In March 1955 the Chief Fire Officer, Joseph Holt, had to go into hospital for an operation and the Fire Service was in the capable hands of Mr. Fradley, the Deputy Chief Fire Officer. In the same month the Fire Brigade was called to Buchanan's Seacombe Mill to deal with an overheated electric motor. Deputy Fire Chief Fradley soon had the motor flames out but decided to remove it and lower it to the ground as a precaution.

Mr Holt received the Queen's Fire Service Medal in July 1955. The ceremony took place in the Wallasey Town Hall when the Lord Cheshire, Lieutenant of Viscount Leverhulme, award to Mr. presented the Holt who was accompanied and three

Mr Joseph Holt

arrived at the scene within minutes and fought the fierce blaze that was over 60ft. from the ground. Flames rose to 25ft. as the Firemen attacked the fire from two sides using the 60ft. Turn-Table Ladder and pouring water through the window of the office. Wearing Breathing Apparatus, the Firemen advanced through the flames with Chief Fire Officer, Mr Joseph Holt, directing the operations. The Men had the fire under control within fifteen minutes. The Catering Manager's office was destroyed. This was the first serious fire at New Brighton Tower. Three Appliances were deployed and in addition, a detachment from the Liverpool Salvage Corps.

Mr. Holt said:-

"If the fire had not been discovered when it was, the whole Ballroom would have been involved and the flames might have spread up the building, as well as below, if they had reached a lift shaft nearby. This would have acted as a flue."

In the Tower Theatre there were always buckets of sand hung on the walls so that an outbreak of fire could be quickly dealt with.

On another occasion, the Brigade was called to the Tower Amusement park to rescue people who were stranded in midair in the small cable cars of the Chair Lift that took people to the roof of the Tower building from the ground below. The cable had come off the runner.

******

by his wife daughters.

Mr Holt had saloon car with Bill Ambulance driver.

Mr Holt was and would hand if a

an Austin (Reg: EOH 840) Jones from the Service as a practical man gladly lend a fireman needed

help in changing a tyre on an appliance. He retired in 1960.

New Uniforms came in 1955 a short double-breasted jacket replaced the Policeman's tunic and the Officers' peak caps had a thin red braid which ran under the crown piece.

In October 1955 a 54 year-old gentleman took ill and died while carrying out a roof repair on his house in Morley Road. Neighbours helped and the Fire Brigade were called. Leading Fireman Dean brought the body to the ground.

Mr PP Booth, HM Inspector of Fire Brigades, carried out the Annual Inspection of the Wallasey Fire Brigade. He watched a Fireman being lowered to the ground from a height in a sling and then inspected all the Appliances with Wheeled Escapes being raised for his inspection.

He said that there was a need for more volunteers.

Chimney fires had increased by 54 compared with the previous year and he pointed out that it was a punishable offence for anyone to set fire to the chimney.

There were 42 outbreaks of fire caused by children playing with matches. It was up to the parents to tell their children the dangers of playing with matches.

In 1956, the men worked a 56 hour week – 24 hours on then 24 hours off. There were three watches: three days on, three nights and three days off.

There were three Pumps at the Fire Station, the 60ft. Pump Escape, 50ft.Bedford Pump

Sergeant Roberts surveys the scene where a passenger is being taken to hospital following and accident caused by two buses colliding at Lloyd's Corner 23 March 1959

Wallasey Fire Brigade taking part in "Audemus Dum Cavemus", a film about the borough. Firemen used a wheeled Escape and 'rescued' a person from a fire in Manor Road

Escape and the Leyland 'Cub' which was equipped with a 35ft. ladder and in addition there was the Turn Table Ladder. The 'Cub' was withdrawn in 1958 and sold to Butler's Garage in Breck Road for scrap. Then In February the students from the Art School in Central Park borrowed it for Panto Week. They dressed up in Firemen's helmets, old and new, for the parade.

There was a gas explosion in a house in Adelaide Street where two ladies lived. One turned on the gas boiler and then looked for a match. The Fire Brigade were summoned to the scene but the house was wrecked.

Accident at Lloyd's Corner

There was a serious accident at Lloyd's Corner involving two Wallasey Corporation buses on 23 March 1959 (*see photo*).
Two buses collided – one hurrying back to Seacombe Ferry for the rush-hour commutors. The No.3 Route bus had clipped the No.14 Route bus as it was coming along Wheatland Lane, causing it to crash over on its side. The Ambulance services and Police raced to the scene. Mrs May Elizabeth Jones, who had been trapped under the bus, along with 14 passengers were taken to Victoria Central Hospital in Liscard Road. Sadly Mrs Jones died a few days later but the others were allowed home after treatment.

In 1959 Mr Holt had a Deputy, 64 full-time staff; 55 AFS men and 14 women. The women were not fire fighters but did administration work and operated the switch board. The Appliances consisted of two Pump Escapes, three Pumps, a Turn-Table Ladder, a TP and a GPL.
The Brigade was continually dealing with grass fires in the hot summers including fires on the Leasowe Estate, Danger Field and other places. When the old steam trains went to Seacombe Station, hot cinders falling from the engine would cause grass fires.

It was in 1959 and 1960, the film "Audemus Dum Cauemus" (as mentioned in the Police Section – Part One) was made. It covered the town's many undertakings including the Fire Brigade where they featured in a make-believe fire which was arranged with smoke coming from a bedroom window opposite the Fire Station in Manor Road. A passer-by telephoned the Brigade, albeit from Church Hill in Wallasey Village. The call was actioned and we see the Firemen descending down the pole to man a Dennis Pump-Escape. Mr. Keith Medley shoots the scene as the Brigade arrive. The Escape is hauled off the Appliance and raised up to the window where a 'casualty' is brought carefully down and taken away in a Daimler Ambulance (*see photograph*).
In November 1959 it was decided that Mr Ernest Edward Buschenfield, Deputy Chief Fire Officer and Chief Fire Prevention Officer at Northampton, would succeed Mr Joseph Holt, who retired after serving as Chief Fire Officer at Wallasey for 12 years.

Big Fire

One of the biggest fires in Wallasey was that of the large grain warehouse at the Flour Mills, Dock Road belonging to the Liverpool Storage and Transit Company. It caught fire on 20 June 1959 with 125 men from all over Lancashire and Cheshire, under the command of Mr Joseph Holt, the Wallasey Chief Fire Officer, fighting the blaze all Saturday night. The Wallasey Brigade raced to the scene at 9.20pm. As soon as the seriousness of the fire was known, re-enforcements were called out to assist them. Some 25 Appliances were used from Brigades as far as Warrington and Chester including six 100ft. Turn-Table Ladders. The bridge linking the blazing premises to another warehouse was extensively damaged and had to be dismantled. Flames leapt a hundred feet into the air from the 800 feet long building which was 14 storeys high. Firemen fought the blaze for over four hours and the Liverpool Salvage Corp. was called in. Cargo ships in the docks were warned to watch out for flying sparks and the Police closed all roads leading to the docks. The AFS helped and the WVS served teas to the Firefighters from their mobile canteen.
While the fire raged, the Brigade received a call at 10.50pm and the standby Engine at the Wallasey Central Fire Station raced down to Gorsey Lane, leaving no cover at the Station. When they got to the place where the fire was reported to be, the Firemen could not find any signs of a fire. It had been a Malicious False alarm.
"It was a terrible thing to happen", declared Deputy Chief Fire Officer Frank Fradley, "If a genuine call had been received while

Mill fire at Dock Road 20 June 1959

Firemen taking part in a 1960s Parade in Oxford Road with both old and new appliances

the station was empty, there might easily have been a disaster." The warehouse fire came under control shortly after 1am. A third of the warehouse was destroyed and damping down went on throughout the week with damage estimated at over £500,000. Mr. Holt said that it was the worst dockland fire for eleven years and had been a very busy weekend for the Brigade which had been called out four times on the Sunday to grass fires at Sea Road, Bayswater Road and twice to the Derby Pool.

Ninety Hours

The men were now working a 60 hour week. If they did six nights of 15 hours this would result in a 90 hour shift. Sunday to the following Monday meant an 84 hour shift

Fishy Story

An unusual Call-Out for Special Services was when the Brigade were asked to come down to the Guinea Gap Baths. There was a display of dolphins and one was sick and had to be taken out of the water. At first the crew were cautious, but once they were assured that it was harmless, the put on their bathing trunks and jumped into the pool and after a short while had the dolphin to the side of the bath. The vet was at hand and discovered that the dolphin was suffering the equivalent to influenza.

Sometimes things would go wrong. The Brigade would be called out to deal with a chimney fire. They would have to hose down the chimney-pot to put it out, but due to faulty brickwork, the water would go down the wrong flue and drench the neighbour's parlour by mistake!

The Brigade have been called out to all sorts of situations, one or two being too embarrassing to relate!

1960s

Manor Road

It is interesting to look at some of the men who were living in Manor Road in 1960.

At No.5 was Sam Pink, Joe Barke was at No.21, Tom Garner at No.6. at No.18 was Edwin Garner and Herbert Winstanley was at No.20.

In 1960, the Brigade was dealing with approximately 900 calls a year.

The Ambulances attended something like 29,500 calls, covering some 150,000 miles.

The Station Telephone number was New Brighton 6154/5.

The Arrival of Mr Ernest E Buschenfeld

But he comes, equipped as suits his station;
He'll give you any further information.

All is prepared, your gallant crew await you.
WS Gilbert

Mr Ernest E Buschenfeld MBE, was appointed Chief Fire and Ambulance Officer in 1960 at Wallasey. He was an excellent Chief Fire Officer and greatly respected by his staff. At the age of 18 he began his career as a part-time Fireman in Kinsgwood Fire Brigade, Gloucestershire. Two years later he became a full-time Fireman

Mr Ernest E Buschenfeld

*Henderson's
store fire
Church Street,
Liverpool
22 June 1960*

with Northampton Police Fire Brigade where he rose through the ranks to Deputy Fire Chief. He was the man that was responsible for modernising Wallasey Brigade being assisted by Mr Frank Uriel.

On 23 February 1960 the Brigade took into its fleet the AEC-Merryweather 100ft TL/P in steel sections was controlled by foot acceleration and could reach the full height in 25 seconds. It was powered by a 170bhp six cylinder engine.

This replaced the 60ft. TL/P. The nine and a half ton Merryweather Hydraulic Turntable Ladder of the 1960s was an impressive machine. The 100ft. steel was in four sections and was mounted on an AEC diesel-driven Appliance (and had a self-contained pumping set and Merryweather single-stage pump which was able to handle 300-400 gallons of water per minute) The ladder was operated from a desk-like console at the rear of the vehicle. The ladder, when closed, could be used as a crane capable of lifting some 2,000lbs. A powerful searchlight and flashing lights were on top of the cab and the Appliance had a chromium-plated bell. A crew of six could sit in the cab. These Appliances can be also used as a water tower.

Henderson's Fire

On a sunny hot day on 22 June 1960 there was a fire at Henderson's store, Church Street, Liverpool. The fire caused serious damage to the building. The fire had been started by an electrical fault. Eleven people were rescued by a Turn Table Ladder from the top floor but 11 died in the blaze.

Twenty-year old Colin Murphy from Wallasey was a ventilation engineer at the store who lost his life in the fire. He had realised that the fans of the air-conditioning were encouraging the flames, so he went back into the flames and made an attempt to switch them off. He helped five girls through a window to safety. Being cut off by the flames himself, he then tried to escape by opening a window to get onto a stone ledge some 60 feet above the

pavement. Smoke and flames burst through the window. Women screamed as they saw him fall to his death.

The Maintaining Manager, Bill Terry, fought the blaze with a fire extinguisher so that the staff could escape. He, too, lost his life. Many Fire Engines were called for from surrounding Brigades including one Pump from Wallasey. Although the Firemen managed to put the fire out in about an hour it was the worst fire on Merseyside since the days of the blitz during the Second World War.

The store opened in temporary premises and an assistant was serving a customer in the blouse department when a Fireman entered in all his firefighting gear. It was too much for the poor girl and she just fainted. She thought there was another fire, instead he was just making a routine check. The store did not reopen in their original building until 1962.

After the tragic fire, measures were taken to strengthen the Fire Regulations by Act of Parliament.

Return of the Old Brigade

The Wallasey Fire Brigade went the full hog for the Carnival Parade in the 1960s.

A couple of old red Horse-drawn Fire Engines were borrowed and three horses hired. Plates bearing the words 'Wallasey Fire Brigade' were screwed to the Engines and the Firemen wore the old polished brass helmets and one or two donned beards. One Sergeant had a row of medals on his tunic; another Sergeant had a pipe in his mouth. Two shire horses in single file pulled one Engine. The Old Brigade would lead the procession, followed by a modern Dennis Pump, the 100ft. Turntable Ladder and a Green Goddess. The Leyland 'Cub' may have also turned out. The vehicles assembled in Oxford Road and joined the parade to New Brighton, via Liscard, Rake Lane and Rowson Street. It was a very colourful procession on a fine sunny Saturday afternoon and was enjoyed by all.

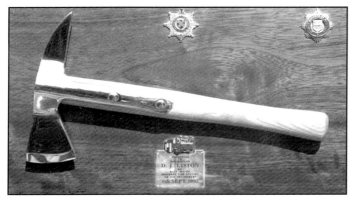

The plaque under the axe reads:
Presented to Sub Officer D.J. Liston Blue Watch Wallasey
Fire Station on his retirement 6th September 1992

Dave Liston Jr.

Fireman Dave Liston was the son of Constable Liston, BEM. He had been keen on body building and was Junior Mr England in his younger days. He went to see Mr. Ormerod, the Wallasey Chief Constable for a reference and joined the Brigade on 10 September 1962. Dave thought that he would not be able to live up to his dad's standard as a policeman, so opted for the Fire Service instead. He went on to become Sub-Officer and retired on 6 September 1992 having completed 30 years with the Fire Service and the Blue Watch presented him with a polished Fireman's axe mounted on an oak board with a plate and badges.

Ambulances

John Smyth was promoted and went to Cambridge Fire Brigade. The Ambulances were painted cream in 1961 and at a later date white, although the older ones remained green and there was a small fleet of saloon cars that were used for transporting patients to hospital or clinics that were able to sit rather than in the need of a stretcher.

In 1962 Ambulance Driver Harold Charles Ellett gained the highest marks in the country in the Preliminary Examination of the Institution of Certified Ambulance Personnel and won the Derek Howarth Trophy and Ambulance Driver Trevor Morgan was also successful in the examinations.

The Steeplechase jockey who rode Frenchman's Cave in the Grand National and racehorse owner, Mr J R Bower, came to the Central Fire Station in Manor Road in 1962 to help to raise funds for the George Holland Testimonial Fund. Liverpool Fireman Holland was suffering from multiple sclerosis.

The 1962 Annual Inspection was carried out by HM Inspector of Fire Brigades, Mr. WE Norwood. The Chief Fire Officer was able to tell him that six women had joined their ranks.

1962 promotions saw G L Edwards become a Station Officer along with Ted Jones and Joe Roberts became a Leading Fireman. In the same year Long Service Medals were presented to Station Officer Walter Meacock, Station Officer Sam Pemberton and Fireman T West.

When Lew Edwards retired he took an appointment with the MTL as a Fire Prevention Officer.

In 1963 The Chief Fire Officer was Mr Buschenfeld, MBE, Mr Frank Fradley was his Deputy. Mr Harold Lacy Fire Prevention Officer and Station Officer with four Station Officers and five Sub-Officers. Three Leading Firemen and 57 Firemen. Mr. Lacey lived at 23 Manor Road. He went on to become ADO in another Division. He returned to the Wallasey Brigade in a similar position to Mr Fradley who had been Acting ADO. The Appliances at the time were a Dennis F12 Pump-Escape, a Dennis F8 Pump, a Dennis F24 Pump Escape, an AEC Merryweather 100ft. Turntable Ladder, an ex. NFS Austin Van, two 'Coventry Climax' 'Feather weight' Portable Pumps. These were driven by a four-stroke, four cylinder water-cooled engine. These pumps were built from 1938 and used in the Second World War. They were capable of producing 214gpm. The Dennis F24 that came into service with the Wallasey Fire Brigade in 1958 was fitted with a 400 gallon water tank and carried foam spray equipment. FHF 60 later served with Merseyside Fire Brigade before being scrapped.

Two 'Alcon' Portable Pumps and one 'Noble' Ejector Pump. The Brigade had 13 sets of Breathing Apparatus sets also one welding and Cutting Set and nine foam making branches.

The Third New Brighton Tower Fire

Fire Engines rang their bells as they dashed along the streets of Wallasey one summer evening. They were heading for the New Brighton Tower where there was a fire in the Social Club on 17 August 1963. The outbreak was spotted by Mr Alex McIntyre, the general foreman. At 7.30pm he saw smoke seeping through the ventilators while he was on his rounds. He raised the alarm

Ambulance pictured in flooded Liscard Road, Liscard

AEC-Merryweather 100 ft. Turn-Table platform with Ted Phillips at the console

School Fire

The Wallasey and Birkenhead Fire Brigade were summoned to a fire that was discovered at 3.25am 11 September 1963 at Barnston Lane Mixed and Infants School which destroyed the assembly hall and a number of class rooms. The school was opened in 1930 and was largely constructed of timber. As the Wallasey crews came down St Hilary's Brow they could see the flames shooting through the roof some three miles away. They arrived at the scene at the same time as the Birkenhead Brigade when the flames were rising to 30ft. into the air. Two more Appliances were called for and under the direction of the Wallasey Chief Fire Officer, Mr EE Buschenfeld and Assistant Divisional Officer H Lacy, seven jets were trained on the burning building. It was hopeless from the start as the centre of the building was one mass of flames and all the Firemen could hope for was to contain the fire and save the extremities of the building. The roof fell in shooting sparks over a wide area. Neighbours were awakened in case they would have to leave their homes. After 45 minutes, the fire was under control and the men continued to dampen down. The Liverpool Salvage Corps helped in the salvage work and 300 children had to be sent home. Mr. KA Rowlands, the Director of Education said that arrangements would be made for the children in church halls and other suitable places.

and on entering the theatre from the club he found it on fire and pieces of blazing timbers and concrete crashing down. After raising the alarm. Mr McIntyre lowered the theatre's safety curtain and asked the early dancers to leave the ballroom. The Amusement Park was also cleared. When the Brigade arrived, he guided the Firemen through the passages making it easier for them to get to the fire. As many as 26 Appliances and 160 men were in action from Wallasey, Birkenhead, Cheshire, Liverpool and Lancashire Brigades.

The fire spread through the canvas ceiling and flames leapt up into the ballroom above. The clubroom and balcony were destroyed. Mr Bill Roberts, the managing director, was able to rescue important records from the office.

The Firemen worked in relays wearing breathing apparatus and managed to stop it from doing further damage. They fought the fire for four hours to stop it spreading to the ballroom and other parts of the large building. Deputy Fire Chief, Mr. Frank Fradley, who directed the operations, said, "At one stage it was touch and go whether the entire building would become involved but everyone did a magnificent job."

Fire Prevention Officer, Mr. Harry Lacy, said that the seat of the fire appeared to be in the vicinity of a television set at the end of the social club.

Mr Fradley praised the general foreman by saying, "Mr McIntyre did a really wonderful job. We were hampered all the time by the smoke and the particular construction of the building, but he acted as our guide. It was a concerted effort by everyone that helped to save the Tower building from being a complete write-off."

He also praised the work of the Liverpool Salvage Corps and the men of all the Brigades, including Mr Bergin of the Highways Department and the manageress of the Lakes Cafe who kindly supplied refreshments throughout the four hour battle.

It was estimated that several thousands of pounds of damage had been done.

*****

A group of ex-Wallasey Firemen

Fireman Ken Harrison who was injured whilst attending a fire at Lucerne Road, Wallasey

This was the third major fire in Wallasey in just over a month. Fire Engines were expected to reach Moreton within six minutes but this was seldom achieved. On 10 August the Leasowe Golf Club house was damaged resulting in damage to the extent of £20,000.

Not So Dusty

Station Officer Tim Riley was with the Wallasey Fire Brigade in the 1960s. He made sure the men were on top of their job and was very keen on keeping the appliances clean. Once he placed a dead match on a Fire Engine to check if the engine would be dusted. He later found it where he had left it and told the Fireman he had not cleaned the appliance properly. "Oh yes I have Sir, I dusted under the match and put it back again!!"

Medals

Alderman Rollins presented medals for resuscitation on Wednesday 1 September 1963 to Firemen B Murdoch, W Walls and K Harrison. He also presented a prize of books to Station Officer Uriel (who had been promoted in the same year) for success in Fire Prevention Examinations.

In 1963 the Wallasey Fire Brigade had a personnel of 78 Officers and men who attended to 1,149 Fire Calls including 230 Special Services Calls, 68 during the severe winter. There was a total of 130 abortive turn-outs by the Police and Ambulance departments. One 18 year-old youth was prosecuted. Other Brigades had assisted on 21 times. A record 1,3002 inspections of properties had been carried out in the year. The Ambulance had carried 39,059 patients over 175,389 vehicle miles – an increase of 2,519 and 19,077 respectively.

The Liverpool Salvage Corps had attended on 92 occasions.

The Wallasey Fire Brigade Ambulance Service Social Club held their Annual Dance at the Capitol Ballroom Club on Friday 11 October 1963.

There was a Call-Out just before 3am to the docks at Lewis's Quay near the Penny Bridge on 1 April 1964. Chief Fire Officer, Mr EE Buschenfield attended with three Appliances and one from the Birkenhead Fire Brigade. A drum of tetrachloroethane was being loaded into the hatch of the Ellerman Line's *City of Swansea* when it burst open. Fumes affected eight dockers and an Officer of the ship's company, who were taken to the Victoria Central Hospital in Liscard and were later released after treatment. The operation took a little over 30 minutes but the Brigade stayed on until 5am to swill away the chemical and clear the lingering fumes in order to allow the loading to restart.

Mr. JW Rothwell was Station Officer at Wallasey in 1964. He had come from Caernarvon Fire Brigade the previous year, originally

Wallasey Brigade attending a Mill fire

Presentation of the Liverpool Shipwreck and Humane Society Certificate to Tom West. Left to right: Ald, John Ashton, Mrs West, Tom West and Chief Fire Officer Ernest Bushenfeld

joining the Fire Service with Liverpool Fire Brigade in 1948. He was with Wallasey for only a short period before going on to Hampshire Fire Brigade as ADO in 1965 and four years later he became Deputy Chief Fire Officer with Dudley Fire Brigade then became Chief Fire Officer with Holland Fire Brigade in Lincolnshire in 1970.

The men were always encouraged to keep fit. On Thursday 4 March 1964 a friendly football match was played between Wallasey Fire Brigade and Southport Fire Brigade at Southport. Wallasey won by three goals to two. Scorers for the local Brigade were Firemen Cook and Harrison with Ambulanceman Lee converting a penalty.

A crew had to dash off from the Annual Parade of the Wallasey Fire Brigade on 5 March 1964 to answer a Fire Call to attend a deep-seated blaze in a refuse dump at Moreton. The Emergency Call had been received while HM Inspector of Fire Brigades, Mr. WE Norwood, was addressing the men after inspecting the parade. He had a special word of commendation for Firewomen Diane Gornall and Hilary Porter for turning out on parade after being on duty all night. He also paid tribute to the work of the Brigade for the year especially in connection with the ballroom fire at the New Brighton Tower. After the demonstration of drills, Mr Norwood inspected the new £19,000 administrative offices next to the Fire Station.

Restaurant Fire

A fire at a fish and chip restaurant in Victoria Place near Seacombe Ferry on Wednesday 22 September 1965 resulted in the owner, Mrs Edith Fairclough, and her 14 year-old daughter being rescued by ladder. Their dog had raised the alarm at 5.15am while they were asleep in the flat above. They smelt burning and soon the house becoming smoke-logged. Opening a window, they called to a workman on his way to work to ring for the Fire Brigade.

The fire raged in the kitchen below, behind the restaurant. A canister of oil was alight with smoke bellowing up into the flat above. Mrs Fairclough and her daughter remained by the window to avoid being suffocated. The Wallasey Fire Brigade soon arrived with three Appliances and Birkenhead Fire Brigade providing another. The Turn-Table Ladder was brought into use with Mrs Fairclough and her daughter, still in their night attire, being rescued through the window and brought to safety along with their four-year-old Corgi, Cheeky.

One evening two Wallasey Ambulancemen had to climb 85ft. up a mechanical crane to reach an injured man at the iron ore berth at Bidston Dock who had been pinned against a stanchion. After reaching the Moreton man they summoned the help of the Turntable Ladder. Norman Stanley Tait was strapped to a special stretcher and lowered to the ground by lifeline from the ladder. He was then taken to the Victoria Central Hospital, Liscard suffering from severe crush injuries.

The Brigade had a busy time in the lead up to Bon Fire Night in 1965. They were called out no fewer than 26 times to deal with bon fires being set off early, in the space of a week.

Mud flats

A father and his two children were trapped in their small speedboat in the mud flats at Egremont one Saturday evening. They were caught between two sandbanks for nearly two hours. A Police Constable had called to them to ask if they had needed assistance but the man said that it would be all right as the incoming tide would re-float them. But high tide was later than he thought and by 8 o'clock he became worried for the children as the light was failing. The Constable returned and again asked him if he needed assistance. This time he agreed.

The Wallasey Fire Brigade was called and using the head lamps from one of their appliances, the 33 year-old Egremont man with his young son and daughter could be seen some 200 yards from the promenade. The Firemen had to work up to their thighs in mud as they brought the stranded family ashore one by one at 9pm. using lengths of wired palings which were laid out to the trapped boat.

Wallasey Fire Brigade attending a fire of stacked deckchairs at Victoria Gardens, New Brighton. From left: Fireman Chas Best, Jim Taylor and Bill Ledder

Wallasey Firemen attending a beached car at the bottom of Sandham Road

Three Wallasey Firemen dressed as Batman, his wonder boy assistant, Robin and the artful Penguin are seen in December 1966 prior to visiting local hospitals

Egremont Tragedy

Wallasey's worst peacetime tragedy was when a grandmother and her five grandchildren were lost in a fire in Egremont.

In the early hours of Sunday morning 8 October 1966 the Brigade was called to a house fire in Guilford Street. A neighbour, Mr Bill Wilson, had spotted the fire and ran to the Sub-Police Station in King Street where 22 year-old Police Constable John Owen was on duty. Together they ran to the small house but could not get in at the rear. They rushed to the front and Constable Owen used his truncheon to gain entry. They were joined by another neighbour, 39 year-old Mr J Fredrick Walker, in the rescue attempt. They crawled into the hallway on their hands and knees but were driven back by the heat of the flames.

The Brigade received the Call-Out at 5am from a neighbour and when they arrived it was too late. They entered the house wearing breathing apparatus. The back living room was burning furiously with flames leaping through the ceiling into the bedroom above. The fire, which was confined to the rear of the house, was brought under control within 15 minutes. However, 52 year-old Mrs Kathleen Joyce Sanders was in one of the bedrooms and had been asleep with two of the children and with the other three grandchildren had died of suffocation. The five children were Paul Alexander Horsley, aged eleven., Dorothy Karen Horsley, aged nine., Julie Amanda Child, aged six., Lisa Maria Child, aged four and Nadine Louise Child, twelve months.

The children's mother 33 year old Mrs Angela Child, a chocolate worker, had been staying with another child in Falkland Road. She was taken to the Victoria Central Hospital in Liscard suffering from shock. Seven Firemen suffered burns: Leading Fireman C Roberts, Firemen R Milne, R Beck, C Best, K Harrison, B Kingey and H Ledder. Constable Owens, who with the neighbour, had made brave attempts but was affected with smoke and refused treatment staying on duty to control the crowds who had gathered at the scene.

The Wallasey Coroner, Mr J Stuart Crooke, commended the efforts of Constable Owen and Station Officer Jack Winstanley. Fire Prevention Officer, Harry Chapman, said that there were several things that may have caused the fire. Mrs. Sanders was known to take a lighted candle upstairs and the switch that was used for the television set was faulty. Clothing could have fallen from a rack in the front-room but the most likely cause was a spark from the smouldering embers in the grate. A chair with clothing on was badly burned.

The neighbourhood and the Brigade were stunned by such a horrific outcome.

******

Fire

A Dutch Barn caught fire at 4am belonging to Catton Brothers in Fender Lane on Saturday 22 October 1966. The Brigade worked under flood lights as they fought the blaze and farm workers used tractors to haul bales of hay away to prevent them catching fire. Some 160 tons of hay was destroyed and damage to the barn amounted to £3,000.

The Chairman of the Fire Services and Licensing Committee, Alderman JC Low, presented Long Service medals in 1966 for 20 years meritorious service to 46 year-old Fireman HC Best. Fireman CW Graham, a 51 year-old married Moreton man with one child also received the 20 years Medal having joined the Brigade in 1946 after serving six years in the Army.

Fireman Ken Harrison was injured whilst attending a fire in Lucerne Road where a pan of fat had caught fire and destroyed the kitchenette. He had gone to ventilate the upstairs floor and cut himself on glass when attempting to open a window which broke. He was taken to the Victoria Central Hospital, Liscard where he had eight stitches inserted.

Batman, his wonder boy assistant, Robin and the artful Penguin of the famous television series were seen running around the Central Fire Station in December 1966 (*see photo*). In actual fact they were three Firemen dressed up as the characters and were off to entertain young patients in local hospitals at Christmas time. They brought much fun and laughter to the children and nurses.

A Fireman poses for the camera in the early 1960s

58

177,000 Miles

The 80-man Fire Brigade had dealt with 407 domestic and business premises, 217 Special Services and 19 grass and heather calls in 1966. They helped 28 people who had locked themselves out and had rescued six cats from roofs, also 2,904 inspections had been carried out during the year. The Ambulance Service had taken 1,700 cases covering 177,000 miles.

Torrey Canyon

The Home Office made a request for volunteers from local Brigades to go down to Devon and Cornwall to assist in cleaning the beaches of oil pollution from the wreck of the *Torrey Canyon* in March 1967. The vessel had been chartered to make a single voyage from the Persian Gulf to Milford Haven with 117,000 tonnes of oil when she went off course and ended up on the Seven Stones Reef and Pollard Rock where she broke in half and discharged 50,000 tons of oil. Firemen Ken Harrison and D Hunt put their names forward and were joined with other Firemen from the North-West. They flew from Ringway Airport to St Mawgen in Cornwall.

Lucky Escape

A young girl spotted the flames from the New Brighton Tower Grounds whilst exercising her dog on the promenade just before the Easter holidays. Two Appliances under the direction of the Chief Fire Officer, Mr EE Buschenfeld attended the incident. Cyril Roberts, a 39 year-old Leading Fireman, had a lucky escape while he was fighting the flames with other members of the crew, when he stepped on a live electric cable. There was vivid flash and he was thrown off balance but was saved from electrocution due to the fact that he was wearing rubber boots. He was very much shaken but continued his tour of duty during the night little worse after his experience. High winds fanned the flames threatening the four nearby kiosks but prompt action by the Brigade saved them from catching alight. The roof of the enclosure was burnt out and the rest of the structure was severely damaged along with ten dodgem cars. Some £2,000 worth of damage was caused to the dodgem cars ride.

More Medals

Long Service medals were presented in 1967. Divisional Officer and Deputy Fire Chief AP Dean had served for 20 years. A married man with four children who lived in Castle Road. He joined the Wallasey NFS in 1947 and transferred to Cumberland Fire Service in 1960. He rejoined the Wallasey Fire Brigade in 1964 as ADO.

Wallasey Fire Brigade Football Team, Winners of the North West Cup 1967/68 Season. Back row - Left to Right: John Dunlop, Bernie Masters, Brian Boyd, Alf Pennington, Derek Redmore, Alfie Gale. Front row: Dave Harland, Jack Wright, Tommy West, Jimmy Joy, Tony Cook. Mascot David West

Leading Fireman JC Roberts, a married man with two children living in Moreton. He joined Cheshire County NFS in 1947 and was transferred to Wallasey five years later.

Leading Fireman A Parker of North Drive was a married man with one child. He had always served at Wallasey and was promoted in 1965.

Fireman RE Phillips had been a Fireman at Wallasey for 20 years and was a married man with two children who lived in Princesway.

Jim Lee retired after 26 years as Senior Watch Room Attendant at Wallasey Fire Station.

In 1967 Fireman WE Corry was presented with the RSPCA's Bronze Medal and Certificate by Vice-Chairman Dr IJM McAllister. The Award was made for 'courage and humanity' during the rescue of three dogs from the River Mersey late evening on 11 May 1967 when the high tide was flowing. Fireman Corry entered the water with a line tied to his waist. After rescuing one dog he went in again with the aid of an extending ladder for the other two animals. The three dogs were in a distressed condition with bleeding paws caused by scratching against the promenade wall. They were taken to a Dogs' Home.

Awards were presented to Station Officer EN Jones, Leading Firemen A Parker and JC Roberts, Firemen GH Smith, J Taylor, and RE Phillips for 20 years service.

Mr Frank Fradley received a Wallasey Council Testimonial for Distinguished Service. He retired as Deputy Chief Fire Officer on 1 April, 1967. He had served in operational duties in the Second World War.

His father, Edward Arthur Fradley, who had been in the Cheshire Constabulary as Constable No.458 was one of the first Constables to join the Wallasey Borough Police (PC.9) in 1913. Both he and Frank served as Police Firemen.

As a young man Frank worked for a dairy and once raced the milk float so fast down Manor Road that it turned over at the bottom of the road! He was a well-liked Fire Officer who lived in Arnside Road and was an elder at Wallasey Village Presbyterian Church.

In the year ending 31 December 1967 the Wallasey Fire Brigade had been called 1,490 times (1,417 times for 1966).

Special Service Calls had fallen from 489 to 301 and with less people having open fires, chimney fires had dropped from 56 to 39. Fires in premises rose from 500 to 581 and grass and heath fires rose from 116 to 179. There had been an increase in Malicious False Alarms from 122 to 175. Three adults and a child had lost their lives as a result of fire. There had been some 177 Call-Outs to fires in derelict buildings. Birkenhead Fire Brigade had assisted on 147 occasions and they had provided cover at the Wallasey Fire Station ten times. The Cheshire County had assisted once and provided cover three times. The City of Liverpool Fire Brigade had also helped out once and provided cover on 13 occasions. The Liverpool Salvage Corps had attended on 98 incidents.

In addition to their normal work, the Brigade also dealt with people getting trapped on sandbanks. This was not helped by the incoming tides and the Fire Chief asked Mr Harding, the General Manager of the Corporation Transport Department, for help. Mr Harding was interested in hovercraft and had developed his own craft 'Wotsit I' and he agreed to help the Fire Service if needed.

The Wallasey Fire Brigade was authorised to have 61 Firemen but in actual fact they had 57. The other personnel consisted of the Chief Fire Officer, his Deputy, the ADO, three Station Officers (should have been four), six Sub-Officers and four Leading Firemen. The AFS had one Station Officer, three Leading Firemen and 15 Firemen. The female staff consisted of one Senior Leading Firewoman and 15 Firewomen.

The Home Office asked for a reduction of personnel to 70 from January 1968. In that year the Divisional Chief Officer, Mr Ernest Bucshenfield, had Mr AP Dean as his Deputy and a full-time staff of 81 (71 men and ten women). The Brigade had a Pump-Escape and three Pumps, a Turntable Ladder, ET, PP5 and a Wartime Emergency Trailer. In that year the Brigade were called out 721 times. 489 were for fires and 25 for Special Services. There were 207 False Alarms.

The Brigade had responded to 1,425 Fire and Special Calls. One child had died from the result of a fire. Fires in buildings had gone up from 581 to 591 and Special Services from 301 to 313. Malicious False Alarms had also risen from 175 to 181.

Assistance from other Brigades for 1968/9 saw Birkenhead helping on 214 occasions while Wallasey Fire Brigade had helped them on 51 Call Outs.

Cheshire County had come in three times whilst Wallasey had helped the County on two occasions. The Liverpool Salvage Corps had attended 68 times in Wallasey.

The personnel at Wallasey for 1968/9 were:-

Chief Fire Officer, Mr EE Buschenfeld, and his Deputy, Mr AP Dean as DO and one ADO. There were two Station Officers for Fire Prevention and three Operational Station Officers. Three Operational Sub-Officers and two Sub-Officers for specialist work. Four Leading Firemen and 53 Firemen. In the Ambulance Service, there was one Station Officer, two Sub-Officers, seven Leading Drivers and 30 Drivers. The female staff consisted of one Senior Lady Firewoman, one Leading Firewoman and six Firewomen. A total of 127. The Fire Service also had ten civilians working for them. In the Ambulance Section there was one Station Officer, two Sub-Officers, seven Leading Drivers and 32 Drivers.

Long Service Medals (for 20 years' service) were presented to B Baguly, G Beck, K Foxley, G Tolond and J Wright in 1968.

Some 2,354 hydrants were inspected and cleaned, 11 repaired, 39 new bonnets fitted as were 68 plates.

The Ambulances covered 180,728 miles, conveying some 49,492 patients.

Alec Dean left Wallasey and went to Westmoreland and came back as ADO and then went into Merseyside as DO and was promoted to SDO.

Bill Parry became Station Officer for the Ambulance Service.

The Rateable Value of the Borough at 1 April 1969 was £3,787,994 and the estimated product of a penny rate for the period was £15,225. The Fire Service was 8.03d. in the pound.

Traffic Accidents

When a Fire Engine is racing to a fire, there is always the danger of an accident.

There was one occasion when the Dennis Pump (HHF 107H) was dashing along Woodstock Road and was negotiating the sharp turn into Love Lane when it met with an accident and ended up farther down the road turning over onto its side on top of a motor car. Luckily no one was hurt and some of the crew boarded the emergency Fender that was following and they continued on to the fire.

Another Dennis Pump (FHF 60) was involved in a crash near the Duke Street Bridge where it collided with a large lorry. Although the Fire Engine was badly damaged no one was injured. Both of these pumps were repaired and returned to service at Wallasey.

The Fourth New Brighton Tower Fire

The New Brighton Tower caught fire on Saturday 5 April 1969. The call was received at 05.08hrs. via the Police Headquarters. The manager of the Tower and his staff had left the building at about 8.30pm after a routine check (the stage area was not included).

The roof of the Tower had been open to the public on the Friday for the first time that year with access by means of the Chair Lift which had been created in 1960 and operated from the ground to the roof.

The New Brighton Coxswain had been awakened by the cracking and banging caused by the fire but after checking all was well in the street, he returned to bed.

Police Constable Edward Brimage was on patrol in Victoria Road at the time and he smelt smoke and set about looking for the fire. He called for assistance and a search was made of Victoria Road and Tollemache Street and by the time that they reached Egerton Street, they discovered that the Tower was on fire in the stage area West tower of the building. It was then that the Fire Brigade was called. The first appliance to arrive was driven by Dave Liston, followed by a second, driven by Walter Peach, the Station Officer. He went to look at the situation and he then climbed the steps to the car park at the higher ground. No sooner had he reached the top when a huge section of the building collapsed. Had he stayed down he would have been killed by the fall of bricks.

It was believed that the seat of the fire was in the stage and the loft. The Brigade had a Pump, a Pump Escape and a Turn-Table Ladder at the scene as well as the general purpose van.

Large bellows of smoke was pouring out of the windows. The Officer in charge radioed: "Make pumps 10 and turntable ladders 2" and placed the van in the car park. The Officer went down the steps that led from the car park to the lower level, made a reconnaissance of the situation and returned to the car park. He heard a crumbling noise and turned to see the whole of the external wall falling. He radioed another message:
"Make turntable ladders 4."

The fourth and final fire at New Brighton Tower on 5 April 1969

Frank Uriel points out the damage to officials attending the New Brighton Tower

The Assistant Division Officer now arrived and took command at 5.20pm with 20 pumps. The collapse of the wall exposed the Ballroom and theatre to the open air and allowing the flames to reach other parts of the building. Things were made worse by the fact that the Tower Boating Lake had been drained and the Fire Brigade had difficulty in obtaining water with Marine Lake by the Battery some distance away. Three relays were put into action. The machines had to pump up the water to the fire, hydrants also fed the Pumps to fight the flames and two Turn-Table ladders were brought into action but with the collapse of the wall it was difficult for the Firefighters.

The Chief Fire Officer, Mr EE Buschenfeld, was now in command and through the lack of water it was obvious that the Ballroom would be a complete loss. Parts of the roof began to fall in. There were some compressed oxygen and dissolved acetylene cylinders in the offices of the fifth floor which were exposed but luckily no one was hurt with the two blasts. Firemen had managed to get into the building from the south but the staircases were impassable due to the debris from the collapsed roof. The Liverpool Fire Brigade were called in with their heavy water unit. Soon after seven o'clock there were 25 Pumps at the scene and further relays were deployed. Further sections of the roof fell in and relief crews were called in from Birkenhead, Liverpool, Cheshire County and Lancashire County with over 150 Firemen being at the scene with 20 pumps and four Turntable Ladders.

Mr Buschenfeld sent for five more Pumps and surveying the situation and the seriousness of the fire, thinking of his men, he shouted to them, "I don't want any heros, let it burn."

Lives of Firemen were more important than bricks and mortar.

The promenade was one mass of Hoes-Pipes and by 9 O'clock fresh crews had to take over but within half hour the fire was under control with crews working on. It was the end of the Tower. In all, 119 Firemen and 37 Officers had fought the fire. There were 25 Pumps, four Turntable Ladders, a Snorkel, a Heavy Water Unit and a Control Unit at the scene. The appliances were refuelled during the fire using up to 313 gallons of petrol, 71 gallons of diesel fuel and 36 pints of engine fuel.

By Wednesday the heap of rubble inside had cooled down sufficiently for an examination to be made but was not possible on account of the condition of the remaining walls. Soon after the fire, demolition work started for fear of children who might try to play in the area with the fairground and grounds being closed off. What caused the fire is uncertain. The Deputy Fire Chief, Mr Alec Dean, said: "A thorough investigation of the cause of this fire was made by the fire department in consultation with the Home Office forensic department and the Cheshire County Police. After the elimination of the possible causes it seems that this fire was due to unauthorised entry to the building and subsequent vandalism or accident in the ignition of the stage area caused by vandals. There could have been no other cause. Electricity and gas had been cut off so these were eliminated and there was no other source. There was a lack of direct evidence to pinpoint vandals but it is the only source that was left ."

The Police had investigated the matter but nobody would come forward with direct evidence. The official verdict was 'Unknown'. By the Wednesday, the heap of rubble had cooled down sufficiently but on account of the dangerous condition of the ruined walls it was not possible to make a thorough examination of the charred shell of the building. Some of the blackened red-bricks started to crumble and steps were taken to have it taken down as soon as possible. Mr Leon Davies, the managing director of the New Brighton Tower, was concerned that youngsters who could venture near the site could be injured or killed. Demolition later took place. Herbert Winstanley (II) of the old Brigade said that if there was a big fire at the Tower they would lose it.

******

'Green Goddesses'

The Wallasey Fire Brigade had, like other Brigades, the famous 'Green Goddess' Pumps. So-called by those who operated them (AFS Appliances being painted green). Their proper name was the Self-Propelled Pumps which were designed for the AFS and although they were of high performance, they required the minimum of skilled maintenance. They were actually owned by the Home Office with a plate stating: 'This vehicle is the property of the Home Office'. They had a Bedford chassis with engines and coachwork by other firms being built between 1953-56 and were capable of carrying between 300 and 400 gallons of water according to the model with a Centrifugal Sigmund FN 4/5 900gpm mounted pump that was fitted at the rear of the vehicle. Each side was 180ft. Hose Reels in addition to the 1,000ft. Delivery Hose. They also had side lockers for various tackle and were heavy machines measuring some 23ft. in length and 7ft. 4 ins. in width. The crew had a cabin (probably the first Engine to have such) with a bench behind the driver and there was a polished brass bell on the left-hand side of the cab with spot and fog lights. Each pump carried an aluminium 35ft. extension ladder with later models being four-wheel drive. These machines were stored on airfields around the country and were checked daily in accordance with the Home Office. They did not conform to the Road Traffic act and were not allowed to go over 30mph. The 'Green Goddesses' were used as cover by the Army during the Firemen's strike.

A number of AFS men learnt to drive in these appliances such as Henry Owen who was a member of the Fire Service after the Second World War.

There were probably no more than two of these appliances in the Wallasey Brigade.

******

Retirement of Walter Peach in 1969. The group includes: Barry Murdoch, Hughie Ross, John McEneany, Ronnie James, Taffy Redmore, Bernie Masters, Gordon Beck, Reggie Font, Billy Agnew, Kevin Foxley, Jack Wright, Jimmy Evans, Ronnie Burrows, Harold Matthews, Tony Cook, Alf Parker, Derek Redmore, Mr Buschenfeld and Mr & Mrs Peach

*Left to Right: Sub O. R Font, Stn O. J Wright, Firemen
K Foxley, D Baguly, S Pink, J McEneany, Unknown,
D Martindale, Clinch, Unknown*

Awards

There have only been two awards for bravery from the Liverpool Shipwreck and Humane Society in the history of the Wallasey Fire Service. This was not because there had been no merited rescues; far from it, but names had to go to the Society for recognition and this seems to have not taken place over the years. Perhaps because Firemen have always taken saving lives as part of their every day work. However, at the Society's meeting on 28 October 1970 it was agreed that Fireman Barry Murdock and Station Officer Frank Uriel should be awarded the Society's medal for courageously rescuing two children from a first floor flat in Cameron Road, Leasowe, Wallasey on 3 April 1970. These two men are the only Wallasey Firemen to receive such awards.

Barry Murdoch retired from the Brigade in 1984.

******

27 Club

The '27 Club' was set up in the old Concert Hall. So called as 9+9+9=27. Ted Phillips became Chairman and on retirement became steward. Much fun was had at the club in the way of Tramp Nights, Old fashioned Nights and even an Hawaiian Night. There were also cabaret evenings. Tom O'Connor when starting out as a young man charged a fee of £15.

Another Dennis

The Liverpool Salvage Corps were operated by the combined insurance companies. Although they did not actually fight fires, they attended and rendered services in such ways as providing emergency lighting and clearing up after the fire.

In 1970, the Wallasey Fire Brigade, purchased a new Dennis F44 Pump painted in the Coventry yellow livery. This Pump was the first Fire Engine to carry the new colour and only two brigades had tried this colour. The livery was used in Wallasey between 1969 and 1973, when the colour scheme reverted to red. The word 'Fire' was painted backwards on some appliances so that it could it read correctly in the motorists' mirrors.

The F44s were the latest Pump appliances in the country. They were built at Guilford and were fitted with a Rolls Royce eight cylinder engine and equipped with twin 180ft. hose reels and had a 400 gallon water tank. They carried a 45ft. aluminium ladder.

With flashing blue lights and twin siren, the Dennis F44 Pump had a Hand-Wheeled Escape which was very successful and was used by many brigades throughout the country The following year, in 1971, another Engine was added to the fleet, being a Dennis F43 Pump. Again this Engine was in the yellow livery. The purpose of this colour was to make them show better at night.

Sometimes a Fire Engine is called a Water Tender Ladder.

Emergency Tenders were sent to the scene of an accident or fire carrying all manner of equipment including First Aid items, breathing apparatus and special protective clothing.

The modern vehicles had breathing apparatus hanging up in the crew cab, lockers holding a large assortment of gear and roller shutter doors which kept out dirt and grime with a rear pump, controls and side lockers.

The modern breathing apparatus consisted of a mask with a large window and a tube connected to the cylinder which was carried on the Fireman's back. This was filled with compressed air.

Some of the older fillings in lounge suites give off poisonous fumes when set on fire. When a Fireman is working in a smoke-filled building he carries a two-way radio set which keeps him in touch with an Officer. A tally with the Fireman's name on is given to the Officer who places it on a board. The Officer knew which men were wearing the apparatus when they went into the building and how much air they had and the time when they should be brought out.

The Dennis Hydraulic Platform (Snorkel) can manoeuvre into positions where other equipment would not be able to do so. The huge folding arm had a platform at the top where a monitor was housed.

The working boom can reach to about 70ft. with an out reach of about 40ft.

Certain fires could not be put out by using water so a Foam Tender was brought into action. This Appliance carried a special high expansion foam generator which drew in the water and was mixed with a special detergent to make the foam which was blown out by a large fan.

Fire Engines all over the country had the same equipment in each locker so that the men could find what they were looking for when other Engines from different Brigades were used on fires.

The Wallasey Fire Brigade responded to 1,689 calls in 1971, which was an increase of 252 on the previous year. Calls to fires were 296; 633 for small fires such as grass or heath; 44 were chimney fires; there were 250 Special Service Calls; 123 Mutual Aid to other Brigades; 116 False Alarms with Good Intent and 218 Malicious False Alarms. Nine exercises were carried out in the year.

One person died as a result of fire compared with four in 1970. Several people were injured whilst cooking in their kitchens.

The Ambulance carried some 46,019 persons (46,053 in 1970). Mr Buschenfield was also the Ambulance Supervisor.

On 11 April 1971 an elderly lady who lived on her own in Gordon Road, New Brighton died when her house caught fire due to an electric fire being too close to her bed. The Firemen found her body on the ground floor near the living-room, having fallen

Dennis F43 Pump Escape in yellow livery (1971)

The Wallasey Fire Brigade on parade in the yard at the back of the Central Fire Station, Manor Road. Marion Rose is in the centre with Margaret West (nee Poole) behind and Joan Williams far right

through the burnt-through floor of the bedroom above.

On 14 June 1971 soon after 1m, a passer-by saw flames at a first floor window of *Grandma's Club and Restaurant* in Grosvenor Road, New Brighton and a call was made at the Control Room and when the Brigade arrived, the whole of the first floor was blazing. The clock tower had collapsed and the roof was on fire with residents having to be evacuated for fear that the 60ft. chimney might fall. The Brigade used five jets including one from the 100ft. Turntable Ladder and the fire was eventually extinguished. The cause of the fire was not known.

The Brigade was called to the No.3 Duke Street Berth on 19 November 1971 when smoke was seen coming from the lower hold of No.2 hatch of the motor vessel *Atlantic Ocean* at about 7am. A flashover occurred and the Fire crews had to be called off. It was a long, arduous task and was dealt with by using high expansion foam with as many as 14 Appliances and 60 men being involved and after 17 hours the fire was brought under control. There was much damage to the cargo and after exhaustive investigation, the cause of the fire was returned as 'Unknown'.

Officers and Firemen totalled 70 and in the Communication Staff there was one Senior Firewoman, one Leading Firewoman and ten Firewomen.

There was a civilian staff of nine, consisting of a full-time cook and two part-time assistants. An Administrative Officer, two shorthand typists and two cleaners.

In 1972, the Chief Fire Officer was Mr Buschenfeld, with Mr AP Dean as Divisional Officer and Deputy Chief Fire Officer. Mr FP Uriel was Third Divisional Officer. Mr DP Kelly was the Senior Fire Prevention Officer.

The appliances consisted of two PE, two P, one TLP and one ET/CU.

Mr EE Buschenfeld reported that the Brigade had dealt with 313 fires; 798 small fires; 31 chimney fires; 266 Call-Out for Special Services and 141 times for Mutual Aid. There had been 126 Non Malicious Alarms and 209 Malicious Alarms. The Brigade had also carried out ten Exercises, giving a total of 1,894.

Mr Buschenfeld joined the Chief Fire Officers Working Group of Brigades that was to form the new Merseyside Metropolitan Fire Brigade. The group was to report on the method of organising the six County Borough Brigades and two County Brigades into one unit.

The new Geriatric Day Hospital meant more work for the Ambulance Service. The Brigade had 12 Ambulance vehicles which carried 51,523 patients, averaging 4,293 per month. The Service was due to be transferred to the National Health Service.

The Brigade was called to the Liscard Central Development just after midnight on 21 June 1972 where a fire had broken out in the Market Hall with the automatic alarm having gone off. Heat and smoke made fire fighting very difficult. The flames were extinguished by two main jets but several small stalls were damaged. At 03.33hrs. on 12 August, the Brigade received a call from the Mersey Tunnels Control to Stone Manganese Marine Ltd. Dock Road where there was a major fire in the canteen and pattern shop. Two Pumps were called to the scene and two Turntable Ladders were deployed.

Eight days later on 29 June a passer-by seeing flames telephoned to say that there was a fire at Pinnington's Garage in Water Street. When the Brigade arrived the entire garage was alight and there was fear that the fire would reach the pumps on the forecourt so jets of water were sprayed over the pumps. On entering the garage, the Firemen discovered that the cock was open on a 250 gallon tank of paraffin and was feeding the raging fire. Four main jets were put into use and the fire was extinguished.

Upon investigation, it was discovered that a forced entry had been made into the building and two youths were later apprehended by the Police and were charged with arson. They

Chief Fire Officer Ernest Buschenfeld shakes hands with Harry Chapman on his retirement, with Mrs Chapman in the middle. Others include: Vincent Lee, Walter Peach, Dave Glyn Jones, Don Kelly, Llewelyn Edwards, Bernie Masters, Hughie Ross and Taffy Redmore

Fireman Dave Jones removes dangerous loose brick from a chimney stack in Silverlea Avenue Wallasey after a storm

were sentenced to Borstal training by the Magistrates Court.

On 30 May 1972 the Brigade was called out at 19.20hrs. by the staff of Buchanan's Blue Cross Mill on the Dock Road, Wallasey when two workers had smelt smoke in the Provender Warehouse. On investigation, one man found a serious fire in one of the storage bins on the second and third floors. Right away he evacuated the building and called the Brigade.

The eight storey building was well alight when the Brigade arrived. The fire was beginning to spread across the conveyor bridge to the compound warehouse and the Officer-in-Charge immediately requested assistance then an attack was made upon the fire. Within 30 minutes the upper wall of the Provender Warehouse had collapsed, damaging the Wallasey Brigade's Turn-Table Ladder, several hoses and other equipment. Only one Fireman was injured in the fall of the wall. The fire was now both spreading to the compound warehouse and the main mill. There were 100 Firemen in attendance at the scene, using twenty Pumps and also three Turn-Table Ladders, Hydraulic Platform and ET/CU to combat the fire which eventually destroyed the building but luckily without loss of life. Water was taken from the docks for the jets.

There was another serious fire in Seacombe. The Controller of the new Mersey Tunnel noticed smoke and flames from the windows of the pattern shop at the Stone Manganese Marine Ltd on the Dock Road at about 0.33hrs on 12 August 1972. By using the direct line to the Fire Station, he informed the Control of the fire. When the brigade arrived at the scene they discovered that the whole of the first floor of the pattern shop and canteen were well alight and the roof was beginning to fall in. Ten Pumps and two Turntable Ladders were called in. The Firemen had to make sure that the fire did not spread to surrounding buildings which were constructed of Robertson's patent galvanised metal sheets which were coated with bitumen on either sides. Five main jets were deployed onto the fire and surrounding buildings using two Turn-Table Ladders monitors, with the fire being brought under control by 04.27hrs. on the same day.

Mr Buschenfeld's Deputy was Mr AP Dean and Third Divisional Officer Mr Frank P Uriel. There were six Station Officers and six Sub-Station Officers, three L/fm and 52 Firemen. Control AGO: F/

Wm and ten civilian staff.

The Appliances at the time were, two Pump-Escapes, two Pumps, a Turn-Table Platform Ladder and ET/CU. There were 12 Ambulances which attended 51,523 calls, averaging 4,293 calls a month.

The Non-Mobile Equipment in the 1970s consisted of three Coventry Climax Featherweight Portable Pumps, two Alcon Portable Pumps, one Noble Ejector Pump, one (later two) Hathaway low Output Floating Pump, five Foam Making Branch pipes, 400 Gallons Foam Making Compound, one Oxygen/Compressed Air Booster Pump for recharging cylinders, one Welding and Cutting Set, one Propane Heater Torch, one Flex-force Lifting Gear, one Electric Generator Set complete with Floor Lights and Power Operated Tools, one Trifor Heavy Towing Equipment, one Portable Cutting Set, and Medium Expansion Foam Equipment.

Mr. Uriel was ADO and became SDO in the Western Division and Mr Noel Stead retired as Merseyside's Assistant Fire Officer. He had joined the Birkenhead Fire Service in 1959 and was promoted to Station Officer in 1970 then moved to Wallasey. He was on duty at the town's biggest fire at Blue Cross Mill. When he was promoted he was presented with a framed photograph of the fire which hung on the wall at the Wallasey Fire Station. Mr Stead retired and his position was temporary replaced by Mr Joseph Killoran.

There were 1,894 Calls in 1972 of which 798 were small fires, such as hearth and grass and 51,523 patients were conveyed by Ambulance.

The Wallasey Fire Brigade had always helped local charities over the years. On New Year's Day, 1973, the Firemen had a pram race through Liscard Village and up Manor Road. One group dressed up as women and others as babies with the prams being draped with material then decorated with silver and coloured paper. Many people lined the pavements to enjoy the fun.

Another time the Firemen dressed up and climbed the steel tower in the Station Yard and came down the Turn-Table Ladder. Jack Winstanley dressed up as an Arab and Chas Best donned a top hat and white beard.

There was a fire at the old Catholic School in Hope Street in 1973, which the Brigade successfully extinguished.

The Brigade was called to a fire in the Tudor Club in the *Tivoli* Buildings, New Brighton, in February 1973. They arrived at 2.15am and Six Engines with 40 men were eventually deployed at the scene with some 200 gallons of water being pumped on the flames for nearly two hours. The roof eventually fell in and Firemen were still damping down the following day. Over £30,000 worth of damage was caused by the fire and the building was demolished in 1976.

Another fire was at Cadbury-Schweppes' factory at Moreton on 4 September 1973.

Frank Feryhough of Bridgecroft Road retired in 1973. He had joined the Wallasey Fire Service in 1941 then became an Ambulance Driver, going on to drive the 'sitting cases' to hospital and was one of Wallasey's longest serving Ambulance men. Alderman Walter Jones, Chairman of the Fire Service Committee presented him with a framed Testimonial.

More than a quarter of the Calls in 1973 were False Alarms – 209 being Malicious. The Brigade had answered some 1,142 in all and 3,240 Fire Prevention visits had been made.

Mr LO Clarke, HM Inspector of Fire Brigades, carried out the Annual Inspection. He said "Wallasey has a very good Fire Service. It's standards are high and its progress good".

The new Head Quarters in Mill Lane were opened on 27 March 1974 by Alderman Walter Jones and on 1 April the Brigade became part of the Merseyside Fire Brigade. The new Fire Station had an

Appliance Room with six bays and had further bays that could house Brigade spare vehicles.

The Station was built on the site of the old Public Weighing Machine (William Pugh used to be the Keeper of the Weighbridge) and Corporation Yard with the tower being situated in the yard. There were two Dormitories, a Drying Room, Mess, Kitchen and Lecture Room and the men could relax by playing snooker or table tennis.

There was a fire at the New Brighton Tower Theatre Club that caused £60,000 worth of damage in September 1974. A burglar alarm was set off by the heat and the Fire Brigade had difficulty in getting past the parked cars in Molyneux Drive. When they arrived they found that the water supplies were poor which hampered their efforts in bringing the fire under control. Nine Pumps from all over Wirral attended and the Firemen were still at the fire at nine o'clock in the morning, having started in the early hours. Police made enquires as there had been two recent fires in clubs at Grandma's in Victoria Road followed by another at the Tudor Club in Tobin Street.

MERSEYSIDE FIRE BRIGADE

The local Fire Brigades were reorganised into the new Merseyside Fire Brigade which came into being on 1 April 1974 with a total of 34 stations under the control of Mr Frank Taylor, CBE, QFSM.

Mr Taylor had been previously in charge of the Liverpool Fire Brigade and when he retired in 1976 he was succeeded by Mr Sydney Rankin who remained until 1983. He in turn was followed by Mr Dennis I Wilmot. Mr Brian Jones was Acting Chief Fire Officer from 1987–89.

Head Quarters are at Hatton Garden in Liverpool and Mr Andrew Best, QFSM, MI became Chief Fire Officer with Mr Michael Sullivan as Deputy. The Fire-Police Station was originally in Temple Court and moved to Hatton Garden in October 1858.

The Chief Fire Officer of the Merseyside Fire Brigade in 2001 was Mr Malcom Saunders.

Mr Buschenfeld

Mr Buschenfeld remained as Chief Fire Officer at Wallasey with Mr Frank Fradley as his Deputy who had a full-time staff of 71 (male and female).

Mr Ernest E Buschenfeld served in the Fire Service for 41 years, starting in 1934 at Bristol, then moving to Northampton in 1938. It was there that he met and married his wife, Freda. For many years he trained recruits and became a specialist in fire prevention, becoming a Station Officer and Deputy Fire Chief in 1955. In 1960 he became Chief Fire and Ambulance Officer at Wallasey where he held the position for 14 years. He was awarded the MBE for his

services to the British Fire Service. With the reorganisation of the Fire Service in 1974 he was appointed Assistant Fire Chief in the Merseyside Fire Service in charge of the fire prevention team. Amongst his recreations he enjoyed home decorating and portrait painting. He retired 31 March 1975 after 41 years in the Fire Service. During the National fire Service he served as Training Officer at No.9/10 Fire Force Training School at Louth in Lincolnshire and went to live in Weston-Super-Mare. His daughter, Wendy, ran a retirement home in Teignmouth, Devon where he went to stay. He had two sons, Nigel and Stephen, eight grandchildren and two great grandchildren. Mr Buschenfeld died in 1993 at the age of 76. The 129 year-old Birkenhead Market was destroyed by fire in 1974 causing two million pounds worth of damage. Fire crews fought the flames for three hours

The Old Rectory of St Hilary's Church was gutted with fire in December 1974 and a second fire occurred two days later on 13 December 1975 in Green Lane and a six year-old died in a blaze. His parents and sister escaped. The Firemen had arrived at the scene at 1.50am.

Firemen's Strike

In May 1977 an unofficial work-to-rule was adopted on Merseyside. Men were told to return to normal working or go home. A large number of Firemen gathered in a field off Strand Road in Bootle and there was a call for an all-out strike. The Chief Officer said that all the men were dismissed but the men said they would continue on strike until all the dismissal notices had been withdrawn. This was the case and the men were told by the Chief Officer that he would accept their date of return to normal work.

In 1977, the Fireman's pay was £65.70 a week.

The first Fire Brigade Union strike commenced on 14 November 1977 and lasted until 16 January 1978.

The men would gather around braziers outside the Fire Stations to keep warm. The National average wage £78.60 basic for a 42 hour week. A young recruit in the Fire Brigade of 19 would receive £52.53, rising to £65.70 when qualified as a Fireman. A married man with two young children, after stoppages, would take home £46.71 for a 48 hour week of nine hour day shifts and 15 hour night shifts.

The men wanted the basic wage plus 10% for their skill and hazards connected with their work. In other words, about £20 a week more. The Government wanted to limit all pay increases to be no higher than 10% which would mean £5.50 to £6.60 extra pay. Firemen did not receive overtime.

In July 2001 there was another strike over plans to recruit civilian staff to senior posts in the Fire Service. The old 'Green Goddesses' were used again.

Manor Road Fire Station closed prior to demolition. The new station opened in Mill Lane 27 March 1974

Some of the Wallasey Firewomen on Parade including: front left Margaret West (nee Poole) and front right Joan Williams

St John's Market in Liverpool suffered two fires. The first was on 25 September 1977 which caused £2m worth of damage; the second was on 17 December resulting in £12m worth of damage. Some 35 Appliances from Merseyside and beyond attended the fire.

James Taylor joined the Fire Service on 3 February 1947 having been demobbed from the Army. He served in the Royal Army Service Corps in general transport and was in the same Corps as Ted Phillips, though he did not know it at this time. Whilst abroad in Italy he asked his uncle (who was in the army with Jim) for a pen friend. He gave him the name of a girl but she already had one. However, she passed his name onto one of her two sisters called Etta. After the war Jim and Etta were married and set up home in rooms in Wallasey, later buying a house in Silverlea Avenue for £500! Jim retired as Fireman with the Wallasey Brigade in February 1977 having completed 30 years service.

With the dissolution of the Merseyside County Council in 1986, the Fire Services from 1 April came under the authority of the Merseyside Civil Defence and Fire Authority.

The Merseyside Fire Brigade covered an area of over 250 square miles with over 18 miles of hose pipe and 200 ladders.

The modern Fire Appliances now use sirens in place of the bell and have blue flashing lights.

The Dennis Appliance of the late 1970s was of the 'RS' design. They were powered by a Perkins diesel engine, had a 500gpm main pump with 45ft. alloy ladder and a 400 gallon water tank. The Appliance was 23 ft. nine inches long, weighed about 11 tons and contained a crew cabin.

The Dennis 'SS' Water Tender was a popular Appliance and similar to the 'D' series.

Fireman Bernard Masters of Manor Road was presented with the Long Service Medal in 1975 and in 1978 he received the British Empire Medal for services to the Fireman's Benevolent Fund. The 51 year-old father of two had joined the Brigade in 1946 and became a specialist in breathing apparatus and equipment for freeing people from trapped cars.

A new Ambulance Station was built in Liscard Road on the site of the old hospital with the old Fire Station in Manor Road, which had served as an Ambulance Station, now being redundant. It remained boarded up for a while and was finally demolished in 1986 and a car park built on the site.

In the 1990s Dennis introduced the 'Rapier' Water Tender which had an automatic five speed gear box and was noted for its road holding. Merseyside Fire Brigade took delivery of a huge Volvo/ Bronto Skylift 28-2 T I in 1993. This Appliance with a combined platform and ladder aerial cost a staggering £400,000. The turntable boom reached a height of 97 feet with a cage at the top, which was fitted with controls as well as those on the chassis deck. The box-frame of the chassis was strengthened to deal with the stresses when in the operational mode and in addition there were four hydraulic outriggers (jacks) which stabilised the skylift. The vehicle measured some 32ft. in length and weighed 22.5 tons.

A Control Emergency Unit carried a large array of fire fighting equipment and other items needed in their work.

The Fire Service, as in the past, dealt with other duties than just fighting fires with road traffic accidents playing a large part of their work. The Brigade had the job of freeing people from the wreckage using special cutting equipment.

One local church had a flooded cellar when there was a leak in the central heating system and this resulted in bringing in the Brigade to pump out the water.

Storms cause trees to fall across the roads which have to be removed. Chimney stacks get blown down and the Firemen remove the dangerous brickwork.

Bonfire Night still caused problems but much had been done by the Fire Brigade to point out to children the dangers from handling fireworks and subsequently there were less injuries. However, in recent times youths have turned to throwing stones at Firemen called out to extinguish bonfires which caused a threat.

There has always been the problem of youngsters trying to get a ride on the rear of the Fire Engine without the crew knowing, not realising the danger. A small video camera could be placed at the rear of the Appliance in the same manner that are fitted to the refuse collecting vehicles enabling the driver to have a view of the rear.

After a road accident involving tankers where their dangerous load had been spilt were dealt with by Firemen sometimes wearing special chemical splash suits.

After the job was completed, a mobile showering unit would be used to wash down the men still wearing their suits to remove all traces of the chemical.

Helmets, which were made of hard cork and covered with fabric, were issued; yellow ones for the Firemen and white ones for the Officers, so that they could be picked out easily.

Yellow waterproof trousers, which replaced the black variety, made it easier for the Firemen to be seen through the smoke. The tunic, trousers, boots and helmet are placed in handy reach for quick dressing. The yellow over-trousers are rolled up and placed over the tops of the boots and the men grab hold of the hoops at the top of boots, pull them on and quickly pull up the trousers slipping the braces over the shoulders. They can finish dressing in the crew cab whilst on their way to the fire.

The boots have re-enforced toe caps and the soles are made to resist chemicals from soaking through. The axes are kept on the Appliance and placed in their sheaths.

When the Firemen are working at the station, they wear blue overalls. The term 'Firemen' is no longer used as there are now both males and females doing similar work, thence the term, 'Firefighters'.

No town in the country can do without the Fire Brigade. Firemen risk their lives to save others and cutbacks are putting Fire Stations under the threat of closure.

Special Services

Two more unusual incidents occurred in 1998 when they were called to rescue a fox stranded on one of the stone groynes at New Brighton. The animal, however, managed to get back to the promenade on his own. The other incident was when a bedridden lady in Moreton called the Brigade in to catch a mouse that was running around her bedroom. It ran under the bed, over the dresser and around the room. The Brigade came and one man went in with a bucket and hammer, leaving two burly men at the door. The little mouse was captured and released in a field.

1998 saw the death of 90 year-old ex-Station Officer Sam Pemberton. On 3 June 2000 the Brigade was called to the Town Hall to rescue six wedding guests who were trapped in a lift which had become jammed between floors. The guests were trying to reach the first floor to witness the marriage of Kristy Robertson and Dean Couldrige at 1pm. Staff had managed to pass cups of water and battery fans through part of the exposed open front of the lift. The wedding ceremony had to be put back. The Brigade arrived at 1.20pm and the Firefighters wound the lift down to the ground floor which released the exhausted guests at 1.45pm.

In February 2001 the Brigade went to rescue a buzzard that had escaped from its home. The bird had become caught in a tree and was being attacked by magpies, close to Moreton Spur. The Fire crew cut the branches before removing the entangled bird and handing it over to the RSPCA.

The heat was so severe that the firefighters' suits actually started to melt whilst attending a fire in Mayfield Road on 5 October 2001. Thirty Firefighters were at the scene and a Platform Ladder was used to hose down on the seat of the flames with the belief that the owner was trapped in the three-storey house. They only found the owner's dog which was brought out and revived with oxygen. The temperature required to melt a Firefighters suit is more than 1,000 degrees centigrade.

Cut-Backs

With cutbacks in the Service, the Merseyside Fire Brigade are now entitled to make a charge for Special Call-outs such as gaining entry to a property for someone who is locked out or in some cases pumping water out of flooded property.

The Mill Lane Station is known as Wallasey Community Fire Station (West 6). Mr. John H Cox is the Assistant Divisional Officer and responsible for the Station. He has 25 years' experience with Merseyside having joined the Merseyside Fire Brigade in 1981, transferring from Clwyd County Fire Brigade. He lives in Wallasey with his family and has been Station Commander at Wallasey Fire Station since 1993. He has also served at other operational stations across Merseyside and is also as a specialist Fire Safety Inspector and says that he learns something new at each incident.

The Merseyside Fire Brigade has five Metropolitan Districts, Containing 26 Fire Stations: Knowsley; St Helens; Sefton; Liverpool and Wirral.

Wallasey Fire Brigade took delivery of a new Dennis Fire Appliance in August 1999, registration number T664 CCK. This hi-tec vehicle has a distinctive livery to assist other road users to see it well in advance.

This excellent Appliance carries 1350 litres of water and has ample room for the men in the crew cab. The other Dennis carries 4000 litres of water. Both have a water gauge at the rear and a glance quickly tells them how much water is left in the tank. Wheeled Escapes are now not used but have been replaced with heavy metal extension ladders. They are fitted with suction pads to prevent them from slipping and it takes four men to handle them. This Appliance and another Dennis Pump (M772 WKC) are the only two Fire Engines at Wallasey.

Retirement group:Lt. to rt: front: Jack Clements, Walter Meacock & Geoff Towland. Middle: Reg Font, Jimmy Evans, Walter Peach, Don Kelly, Ernest Buschenfeld, Bob Evens, Harold Cash, Frank Fradley, Frank Uriel, Bill Whitfield. Back: Jim Taylor, George Bateman, Noel Stead, Chas Best, Ronnie Beck, Les Derbyshire, Jack Wright, Sam Pemberton, Joe Williams & Les Edwards

There is also a Foam Unit and a Control Emergency Unit. Either can fit onto the back of the Prime Mover (H 653JKF).

Mr Cox has 61 men under his command made up of four Watches that cover Wallasey 24 hours a day on Continental shifts, each having a Station Officer in charge. They are Red: Alan Bridle; White: Ken London; Blue: Ian Hammond and Green: Tony Buratti with the Green Watch being an additional one. Each Watch has a Station Officer, one Sub-Officer and one Leading Fireman with a total of 15 men on a Watch.

The Community Fire Safety Officer is Barry Allen who works with local schools and firms to encourage Fire Safety while Kevin Phillips is in the Wirral Community Fire Safety Department, who visits schools to present the safety aspect to prevent fires and answers questions from the school children.

A team of Firefighters from Wallasey scaled the heights of Mont Blanc in Southern France in 1999. The intrepid trio from Red Watch were sponsored by their colleagues at the Station. Green Watch entered a team of six in the Three Peak Challenge which had to climb three different 'hills' over two days.

At the time of writing, the Wallasey Fire Brigade can boast no fewer than three rugger players. Ian Kennedy, Lee Hodges and John Shuddal. All three used to play for New Brighton at Reeds Lane but have now joined Birkenhead Park.

'Duck the Fireman' has been a popular fund-raiser for quite a time. In 1993 this light-hearted event raised a grand total of £9,00.

An old milk float has been donated by Express Dairies (who also maintain the batteries and supply spares). This has been made into a sort of bus which is used at fetes and other events. It has seats for about ten children and is used to transport them at 20p a ride. This vehicle can be hired out for community shows.

All Watches take part in various fund raising events. Over the years, Fire Fighters have raised thousands of pounds.

A joint effort with the Police has combined to put on a children's show at the Floral Pavilion which costs £7,000 to produce. The money is raised by car washes etc. and the remainder is made up by sponsorship.

The Fire Service Benevolent Fund is well supported by the Wallasey Station crews. They have raised over £5,000 at the time of writing.

In 2001 new Ambulances took to the streets of Merseyside and Cheshire. The new vehicles have the design of green and yellow quarters, replacing the cheron stripes. The Ford Transit Ambulances cost £50,000 each and carry the very latest equipment.

Advice on fire Prevention

Chief Fire Officer of Merseyside Fire Brigade, Malcolm Saunders has set a target in reducing the number of fatalities. A five year plan has been set up with the hope of reducing the deaths in fires by 40%, injuries by 5% and house fires by 33%. Some of the ways to achieve these figures included: a campaign to encourage residents to have a smoke detector installed in their homes; school visits; lectures and home risk assessments.

The aim of the Home Fire Risk Assessments is to provide every home on Merseyside with the opportunity to have a visit from the Fire Brigade with a genuine attempt to create a safer community. Where there was a risk of fire, the Brigade will give advice or fit smoke alarms, making a return visit within twelve months; lesser risk will just give advice and, where necessary, in a medium to low ratings, the Brigade would return within five years. At the present time, the Brigade will visit any home in Wallasey and carry out a free Home Safety Check and fit a free smoke detector. I hope that readers will take up this offer by telephoning 630 3040.

Every home should have at least one smoke alarm. These are reasonably priced and two or more is ideal. One should be placed on the landing and the other somewhere near the kitchen and living-room.

It is very important that the battery in a smoke alarm should be replaced immediately the signal indicates the battery needs replacing. Failing to do this can cost lives.

One should make sure that gas or electric fires are turned off before retiring for the night. The same applies to cookers. When a frying pan catches alight it is dangerous to throw water on it. A large damped tea towel or such should be thrown over the pan to smother the flames.

Money is well spent on investing in fire blanket and a fire extinguisher. All bedrooms should have an openable window so that could use it as a form of escape should the house catch fire.

Any reader in Wallasey who needs advice on home safety should not hesitate to telephone 638 0961 and a member of the Fire Brigade will be only too pleased to give advice.

Remember:

In the event of a fire use this procedure:-

First: Raise the alarm.

Second:,   Evacuate the premises immediately.

Third: Dial 999 and call the Fire Brigade.

**Do not stop in the premises to collect valuables
and only tackle a fire if it is safe to do so.**

******

APPENDIX I

Police Officers

It is to be understood that all Officers started their Police career as Constables. Those who joined from Police College and became Inspectors also did a period as Patrol Constables.

As regards the Fire Service, the majority started as Firemen; some as Policemen.

Official lists of Police Officers do not seem to exist. I therefore apologise for the large number omitted and any other errors especially initials and spelling of names.

The dates refer approximately to when the person either joined or the period in which they served.

Chief Constables of Wallasey Borough Police

1913-1930	Percy Linnel Barry.
1930-1959	John Ormerod, BEM, OBE, CBE.
1959-1967	Walter Marshall.

Police force in the 1800s:-

Inspector William Watson, became Superintendent of the Division.
Inspector Rowbottom.
Sgt. John Edward Hindley, became Superintendent for North Wirral (Wallasey). Became Chief Superintendent of Cheshire County.

Sgt. Cooper.	PC126 Thomas Percival.
Sgt. WG Skiff.	PC. 129 Samuel Threadgold.
PC. 94 Patrick Keenan.	PC. 138 William Duffy.
PC. 96 Samuel Heaps.	PC. 204 Potts.
PC. 99 John Hindley.	PC. 301 Jones.
PC. 103 Thomas Hindley.	PC. Edward Dodd.
PC. 103 Anthony Ibbotson.	PC. Robert Lea.
PC. 104 Thomas Duffy.	PC. Mealor.
PC. 112 Joseph Millington.	PC. Mullins.
PC. 117 WJ Samuel Horne.	
PC. 121 George Parker.	

One of the two Duffys was later given the number 7.

1900 onwards:-

Superintendent Richard S McDonald-followed by
Superintendent John McHale.
Insp. Thomas J Morris (From County), became Chief Inspector.
Acting Sgt. Hugh L Kenny, became Full Sergeant.
Sgt. A Phillips (County Sgt.396), Killled In Action.
Sgt. Arthur Sandland (County Sgt.74), became Chief Inspector.
Sgt. William Thompson.
Sgt. Joseph D Venables.
Acting Sgt.G Sawage (County PC.322).
PC. 38 William Barber (County PC.485).
PC. 54 Joseph William Barke.
PC.   Walter Barke.
PC. 32 Wiliiam James Batty.
PC.   Alfred Astbury Bebbington (County PC.507), became Sergeant 14.
PC.   John Bebbington (County PC.418), became Inspector.
PC. 18 Herbert M Bland.
PC.   C Bland (County 275).
PC. 6 Martin Brenman (County PC.329). Went into CID.
PC.   John R Bryan, became Superintendent.
PC. 25 Edward Gilbert Burgess. (County PC.72) Resigned.
DC.   K Cartwright (County PC.242).
PC.   L Currrell.
PC. 23 David Dawson (County PC.473), became Sergeant.
PC.   RK Darkeley, K.I.A.
PC. 13 John Davies (County PC.2).
PC.   Charles Herbert Emsley.
PC.   GB Fairhurst (Conuty PC.457), K.I.A.
PC. 7 Henry Farran (County PC.444).
PC. 9 Edward Arthur Fradley (County PC.458). Also Fire Brigade.
PC. 21 William Griffiths (County PC.180).
PC. 30 William Henry Hallam (County PC.351).
PC. 35 John Robert Hesketh (County PC.11), became Sergeant (Later Reserve Constable R6)
PC. 12 Walter Jackson (County PC.180).
PC.   Edward Ferris Jones (County PC.62).
PC. 28 John Latham (County PC.19).
PC.   Thomas Latham (County PC. 221), became Sergeant 9.
PC.   Matthew Leigh (County PC.297), became Inspector.
PC.   William Lidgett, (County PC.22), became (Sgt.10) Inspector.
PC.   John Burgess Lockley (County PC.371), became Sergeant.
PC.   John William Marshall (County PC.227), K.I.A.
PC.   John Molyneux (County PC.299).
PC.   Walter F.Newbrook (County PC. 255).
PC.   W Nelson (County PC.7).

PC. W Nutt (County PC.67).
PC. John O'Reilly.
PC. Edwin Pearse.
PC. Robert J Pearson (County Sgt.419), became
Superintendent. Later Chief Constable of Cambridge in 1919.
PC. 37 John Pickford (County PC.469).
PC. Walter Smith Price.
PC. 31 William S Price (County PC.499).
PC. William Henry Price.
PC. TW Roberts (County PC.189), became Det.Inspector,
became Superintendent.
PC. FA Robinson (County PC.24).
PC. George Savage. Joined in 1900, left Wallasey Force.
Returned 1913 became Sergeant.
PC. E Fredrick Scott (County PC.328).
PC. T Shore (County PC.448).
PC. WGG Short (County PC.293), beeacme Sergeant 4, later
CID.
PC. James Smith (County PC.201), became Sergeant.
PC. 26 Douglas Percy Swetman (County 226).
PC. 33 George Taylor (County PC.465).
PC. 24 William Tomlinson (County PC.462), became Sergeant.
PC. 39 Richard John Thompson (County PC.10).
PC. William Tomplinson, became Sergeant.
PC. 10 David Tweadle (County PC.382).
PC. 120 John Wainwright became Sergeant.
PC. 27 Walter Webb (County PC.486).
PC. John Wedge (County PC.188), became Sergeant. Went into
CID.
PC. 76 Herbert Winstanley, Fire Brigade, became Sergeant.
PC. J Winstanley (County PC. 248).
PC. WC Wood (County PC.437).

Added in Circa 1913 – Second World War:-
Chief Constable Percy L Barry.
Insp. Richard Stanley Bennion.
Insp. SF Butler, became Superintendent. Chief Constable of
Ramsgate 1916.
Insp. Thomas Ennion, became Superintendent of Wirral Division.
Insp. Hatton.
Insp. Mathew Keigh.
Insp. John Lees.
Insp. R McDonough, KIA
Insp. Thomas J Pears.
Insp. Thomas Phillips.
Insp. William Henry Woodcock.
Fire Officer William Nicholson.
Sgt. 8 Joseph (Joel) Atkinson, Fire Brigade.
Sgt. John Fred. Beere, became Inspector.
Sgt. 2 Samuel Brown.
Sgt. Robert Collins.
Sgt. William Davies.
Sgt. Joseph Holt, Fire Brigade, became Fire Chief Officer.
Sgt. A Keafe (Tax Officer).
Sgt. Keen.
Sgt. 5 Alexrander Keith, became Det.Inspector.
Sgt. WA Leggett.
Sgt. 6 Walter A Payne, became Inspector (GEO).
Sgt.11 Thomas Wilkinson, Fire Brigade.
Sgt. William Crook Whiteside, became Inspector.
Sgt. 3 Fredrick E Wood.
Sgt. 1 Herbert Worrall.
PC. Richard Aldridge.
PC. Victor Alexander, Fire Brigade.

PC. Silas Allman.
PC. Joseph Knowles Andrews, became Sergeant.
PC. 56 William Henry Anderson, became Det.Inspcector.
PC. JH Anderton, KIA
PC.103 John Armstrong, became Sergeant.
PC. 53 Heber Ashall.
PC. AJ Barnaby, Fire Brigade Ass. Motor Engineer.
PC. 14 James Banks.
PC. 2 Eric Barke, went into CID.
PC. John William Barke.
PC. Bradley.
PC. 59 William Basset.
PC. 77 Thomas Bate.
PC. 78 Thomas Beresford.
PC. 42 Henry Benfield, Fire Brigade.
PC. Henry G Bernard.
PC. George Robert Benfield.
PC. John Bennet.
PC.100 Leonard Hamilton Bliss.
PC. Bowery, became Acting-Sergeant.
PC. JG Bradley.
PC. 6 Martin Brennan, went into CID.
PC. CE Brown.
PC.111 Herbert S.Brown, became Sergeant.
PC. Harry Sidney Brown, became Chief Superintendent and
Deputy Chief Constable.
PC. JD Brown.
PC. H.Burrows.
PC. John Cain (later PC.22).
PC. 5 Lawrence Carroll (County 215).
PC. Kennth James Cauldwell, became Det.Inspector.
PC. William Bert Clague, Fire Brigade. Had served as a Wallasey
Constable prior to First World War.
PC. 3 William George Craft.
PC. William George Cripps.
PC. 15 Monty Caugherty.
PC. 86 Harold Francis Cash, Fire Brigade.
PC. 69 George Henry Chilton.
PC. H Clay.
PC. 29 Alfred Cotton.
PC. Robert Collings, became Sergeant 7.
PC. 19 Fredrick William Cooke.
PC. Joseph Cumberland.
PC. James Albert Davies.
PC. David Dawson.
PC. Joseph Henry Dolan.
PC. 57 Henry Joseph Dolan, Fire Brigade.
PC. 83 Sidney Digman.
PC. RK Drakeley, KIA.
PC. Herbert Dunn.
PC.102 Robert J Edwards, became Inspector.
PC. Thomas 'Taffy' E.Evans.
PC. 17 William John Evason, Fire Brigade.
PC. AR Fare, KIA.
PC. AM Farquharson, KIA.
PC. George William Fidler (later PC.32).
PC. 45 William E.Field.
PC. Stanley Fisher, became Chief Superintendent.
PC. 30 Leslie Fisher, brother of the above.
PC. Frank John Fradley, Fire Brigade.
PC. Charles Joseph Gibson, became Det. Chief Inspector.
PC. 71 Micheal Golden.
PC. William Goulding.
PC. 49 Harold Le Grice.

PC. 16 James Gallagher.
PC.   William Golden.
PC. 33 James Edwin Griffin.
PC.   R Ellis.
PC. 73 Thomas Haigh.
PC.   Alan Hamilton (Community Relations Officer).
PC.   Harry Hargreaves.
PC.   Edward A Harrison.
PC.   John A Harrison.
PC.   Leonard E Harrison, became Inspector.
PC. 67 Robert Francis Herron, Fire Brigade.
PC.113 Hugh Henderson, KIA.
PC.   William Henry.
PC. 60 Thomas Highton, Fire Brigade.
PC. 94 Norman Hill.
PC. 55 Stanley Hill.
PC. 75 George Hodges, became Sergeant 8.
PC.   Horder.
PC. 43 John Thomas Holmes.
PC. 92 John Hughes.
PC. 52 John 'Chummy' Ingham.
PC. 99 Alexander 'Jock'Ingram.
PC.   Allan Jackson, Fire Brigade.
PC. 89 Robert Henry Jackson.
PC.   Richard Bertram Johnson, Fire Brigade.
PC.   Neville Johnson, later PC.76
PC. 51 Arthur Davies Jones.
PC.   CE Jones, K.I.A.
PC.   Robert Jones (One became Chief Inspector).
PC. 44 Robert Jones, Fire Brigade.
PC.   William Jones.
PC. 74 William Ernest Jarrett, became Sergeant.
PC. 88 Thomas Kenyon, went into CID.
PC.   George Kingham
PC.   Thomas Lamb.
PC.104 Thomas Henry Lang, went into CID, became Det.Chief
       Inspector.
PC.   M Lea, became Inspector.
PC.   Matthew Leith.
PC.   David John Liston, MBE. (Later PC.7).
PC. 20 Sydney Lodge.
PC.110 J Louis McCormack, became Inspector.
PC.   Michael McDonough (Sgt.12), became Superintendent &
       Deputy Chief Constable.
PC.108 Frank McEvoy, (Resigned).
PC. 50 William Machill, later Sergeant.
PC.   John McHugh (Police Clerk).
PC. 63 Albert Mackey, later PC.118. Became Instructer & Acting
       Insp.
PC.   J Maddocks.
PC. 40 Ivan OGT 'Bud' Maddocks, Fire Brigade.
PC.   J Malone, Fire Brigade.
PC. 47 John Henry Mann.
PC. 22 Leonard F Marsden, Fire Brigade.
PC. 91 John 'Gunner' N Marshall, Fire Brigade.
PC.   Walter Marshall, became Chief Constable.
PC. 93 Thomas G.Minor, became Sergeant.
PC.   Albert Morgan.
PC.   SG Morris.
PC.   Reginald C Myles, Cycle Patrol (later PC.61).
PC.101 Walter Newall.
PC.   Arthur Thomas Nichols.
PC.   Thomas George Nicholls.
PC. 46 John Fitzroy 'Rex' Norris, Cycle Patrol and later CID.

PC.   John Ormerod, joined in 1919 became Chief Constable.
PC.   William Wingfield Partington.
PC. 25 William James Packer, Police Clerk. or packer.
PC.   John Palin, became Sergeant.
PC.   Walter George Peach, Fire Brigade.
PC.119 Kenneth Pearce, KIA.
PC. 64 Lot Pearce.
PC. 34 Edward Pearce (County PC.323).
PC. 98 Frank Peck, went into CID, became Inspector.
PC. 62 William Pender.
PC. 72 Edward V Petherbridge, became Sergeant (Traffic &
       Coroner's Office).
PC. 84 Bernard M Phillips.
PC.   NB Phillips.
PC.   JW Potts, KIA.
PC. 66 David Prendergast.
PC. 87 Edward Prescott.
PC. 31 Thomas Price.
PC. 48 Steven Prideaux.
PC.   John James Read.
PC   John Leslie Read.
PC.   L Reavil.
PC. 11 Arthur Reece, became Sergeant.
PC. 95 James John Reid.
PC.109 W Ernest Reynolds, became Superintendent.
PC.   Robert Richardson, became Inspector.
PC. 81 William Rigg, became Sergeant.
PC.   Joseph (Tim) Riley, Fire Brigade.
PC.   Thomas Riley.
PC.   George Roberts, Fire Brigade.
PC.   Peter Coulthard Roberts.
PC. 65 Joseph Ryan.
PC. 46 Charles T.Sandland, became Det.Superintendent & Deputy
       Chief Constable.
PC.   Arthur William Say, Fire Brigade.
PC. 82 George Edward Sharples.
PC.   EA Sharples, KIA.
PC. 68 Walter Shelton, later Det Constable.
DC.   William Sheldon.
PC. 97 Thomas Simm.
PC. 96 Ernest Victor Smith.
PC.   Walter Smith.
PC. 97 Thomas Simon.
PC. 41 David Norman Starkey.
PC. 46 James Steel (resigned).
PC.   William Harold Steele.
PC.   GH Steele.
PC.105 Hugh Grant Stevenson.
PC.   Edward Street.
PC.112 Walter Louis Thacker, KIA.
PC.106 Anthony Thompson.
PC. 70 Jonathan Thorley, Fire Brigade.
PC.115 Richard Waft, became Sergeant 2.
PC.   WD Wagstaff, KIA.
PC.120 Douglas Anthony Wainwright.
PC. 80 George Walker (Mounted).
PC. 85 William George Walker (Mounted but not related to the
       above).
PC.   Eric Walker. (later PC.89).
PC. 61 James Warner Fire Brigade.
PC.   Ernest Warrington, became Inspector.
PC.   TG Wearing, KIA.
PC.   Richard Webster, Fire Brigade.
PC.   ASI Wedgewood.

PC. 58 William Allan Wesley.
PC. 8 Edward Whitticker.
PC. Henry Whittingham (joined the Malayan Police).
PC. L Whittingham.
PC. 79 Alfred Williams, became Inspector.
PC. Douglas Williams, became Sergeant.
PC. 4 John Henry Williams (Mounted), Fire Brigade.
PC. W Williams.
PC. George Winstanley.
PC. William Henry Woolley, became Inspector.
PC. Frederick Egremont Wood, became Sergeant.
PC. Thomas Woodward.
PC. Arthur Wormald.
PC. H Wright, became sergeant.
PC. 64 Alexrander Yule, became Det.Inspector.
PC. EJ Young.
PC.114 Thomas Youmg.
Thomas Lowe, Police Court Commissioner.

* K.I.A. = Killed In Action.

Post 1939-45 World War Two to re-organisation in 1967.
Superintendent W.E.Reynolds.
Insp. C Bowden.
Insp. J Hand.
Insp. DB Humphries.
Insp. Robert E Hughes, became Chief Superintendent (Ex.County).
PC.116 (Sgt.8) Albert Kennedy, became Det.Superintendent in the Cheshire County.
Sgt. Hugh Laughland.
Sgt. JE Lewis.
PC. William Gerard ('Ginger') Adams, became Inspector.
PC. 99 Thomas Abbott.
PC.118 Frank Allman.
PC. Christopher Allen.
PC. 11 Robert Anderson, Traffic.
PC. J Andrews (Probationer; left Force in 1958).
DC. Ernest Atkinson, became Sergeant.
PC. 48 AGD Bailey.
PC. Joseph Barke Jr., became Seageant.
PC. 18 Maurice A Barnes, became Sergeant 5.
PC. 82 Henry Beaman.
PC. John Bennett.
PC. Walter Bennett.
PC. 49 Richard ('Dickie') Bird (Motor Patrol).
DC. John Alex Bowden, Warrant Officer.
PC. 47 John Bradbury, went into C.I.D.
PC. Edward Brimage became Coroner's Officer.
PC. 8 Henry Sidney Brown, became Superintendent.
PC.104 Herbert Brush.
PC. Robert William Burton.
PC. John Carlisle, became Sergeant.
PC. BR Carpenter.
PC. Cocker, became Inspector.
PC. Donald James Collingwood Clarke, became Chief Inspector and Prosecuting Officer.
PC. David Chaddock, became Sergeant 1 (Sec. Retired Police Ass).
PC. Joseph Chamberland.
PC. 16 Kenneth Carter (Dog Handler).
PC. P Coles, became Sergeant.
PC.128 Robert J Collister.
PC. JB Currie (resigned in 1958 to take up other employment).

PC. 65 John Dalton.
PC. Donald F Dransfield, becamed Chief Inspector, Cheshire County.
PC.114 Emrys Edwards.
PC. 42 George CA Edwards (Coroner's Officer).
PC. PH Edwards.
DC. 23 David Craig Evans.
PC. 25 John Farnworth.
PC. Brian Faulkner, became Chief Inspector.
PC. 81 John Fearon, Traffic Dept. Transferred to CID.
DC. J Fearson.
PC. Rowland ('Rollo') P Field (Emigrated to New Zealand in 1958).
PC. George Field.
PC. Elliott Hedley Fisher.
PC. R Fisher.
PC. AS Fletcher (Resigned in 1958 to take up other employment).
PC. Samuel Riverier Foster became Sergeant 12.
PC. 1 Christopher Garvey, Motor Cycle Patrol.
PC. 74 W Gibson.
PC. 51 Stephen Goodhall.
PC.121 John Green.
PC. 5 John Hancox.
PC. 35 Norman Hartley.
PC. P Norman Harvey.
PC.113 Eric Hawker.
PC. 85 Alec Hetherington.
PC. 54 CDE ('Mick') Heenan, later CID & Photographer.
PC. 68 Donald Hesketh.
PC. 44 Harry Hesketh, became Sergeant.
PC.127 Kenneth R.Halliday.
PC. PN Harvey.
PC. 56 William P Holmes, Became Inspector.
PC. 39 Dennis Holmes, became Superintendant.
DC. Leslie Horricks, became Det. Sergeant.
PC. 92 Kenneth Hughes.
PC.107 W.E.I.Huntington.
PC. 78 Jeff Kehoe.
PC. 53 Harold Kelly.
PC. John Kelly, became Sergeant 19.
PC. King.
PC David Kinnear.
PC.119 Douglas Knight.
DC. Peter Lakins.
PC. H Laugham.
PC. 60 Gerald Lee.
PC. AW Lewis, became Inspector (came from Birkenhead Police).
PC.108 Edward Lewis.
PC.115 Raymond E.Lewis (Acting Sergeant and cousin of AW Lewis).
PC. Leonard Littlewood.
DC.112 William Russell Lloyd.
PC. Eric S.Lowe, became Superintendent.
PC. Norman Lowe.
PC.138 Robert F.Lowe, later CID. Became Det. Inspector.
PC. 38 Herbert Wallace Lavery.
PC. 12 Rowland ('Rolly') Lyon.
PC. Wilfred Marsden, became Det. Chief Inspector.
PC. Cecil Cairns Marshall.
PC.113 Anthony William W Martindale.
PC. 19 Eric Marshall, Prosecution Dept.

PC.103 Alec May.
PC. 84 Raymond Molyneux, became Sergeant.
PC.101 TG McCabe.
PC. 26 Robin McCombe.
PC.137 HC MacMillan.
PC.125 Walter Morgan.
PC. 4 Albert Morgan.
PC. 17 TE Morley.
PC. George Moss, became Sergeant.
PC. 80 Thomas Murphy, became Sergeant in Liverpool City Police.
PC.97 Gordon Musson.
PC. 62 JC Mutch.
PC. 77 John E Nance.
PC. 21 RM Newley.
PC. Joseph D Newton.
DC. Peter G Milne, became Inspector,
PC.134 John E Morris (Joined Hampshire Police as Inspector).
PC.121 John Morris.
DC.124 Patrick G O'Dwyer, became Inspector and Prosecuting Officer.
DC. Roberts.
PC.116 D Owen.
PC. John Allan Owen.
PC. 37 James Leo Owens, became Sergeant & Head of CID in Wirral.
PC. E Parker.
PC. 40 Norman Palethorpe.
PC. 88 Donald Palin.
PC. R Parry.
PC. 59 Alec Paterson.
PC. 87 Thomas Paterson.
PC. Thomas Pearson.
PC. Arthur William Peachey.
PC.123 Dave Physick.
PC. 28 James Pinder.
PC. Peter A Pinnington.
PC. 29 Charles Potter.
PC. 93 Cyril Rae.
PC. B Roberts.
PC. Richard Rhind.
PC.105 Allan Rickett.
DC. Alan Rimmer, became Det. Inspector.
PC. Geoff Roberts, became Sergeant 6.
PC. Brian Rogerson.
PC. 27 Stanley F Rothwell, became Sergeant.
PC. 58 John Rutter.
PC. 70 John Shakeshaft.
PC. G Sharpe.
PC. Charles Shires.
PC. Alan Smith.
PC. Phillip S.Smith.
PC. SH Smith.
PC.135 G Stokes.
PC. Ronald Squires, became Sergeant. Motor Patrol.
PC. 72 Edward Stanley.
PC. Alan Steen.
PC. JR Steen.
PC. Allan Stockdale.
DC. Leonard A Stocker, became Det. Inspector.
PC. EE Sutton (Resigned to take up other employment).
PC.122 George H Smythe.
PC. 95 Kenneth Tonge.
PC. Maurice E Toyn, became Inspector.
PC. Arthur Trowell, became Sergeant 9.

PC. T Urmston, attached to the NFS.
PC. Eric Leslie Valentine (Drowned whilst on Duty).
PC. 57 Alan Walker, became Sergeant.
PC. Eric Walker, Cycle Patrol.
PC. 20 FA Walker.
PC.102 Donald Watson.
PC 110 James Watson.
PC. Kenneth Watson (One Watson became a Sergeant).
PC. 34 Tony Weston, became Inspector in the CID.
PC. RE White (Joined the Navy in 1958).
PC.129 Leslie T Whitfield, became Superintendent.
PC. John Whitfield.
PC. W Whitfield.
PC. 67 Roy Wilcox, Dog Handler.
PC. Alan Wilkes.
PC. Alan Williams.
PC. 50 Douglas D Williams.
PC. ET Williams.
PC. T Williams, became Sergeant.
PC. 49 Henry Wood.
DC. 63 Vernon Young.
PC. 96 RA Young.

Women Police Constables

WPC. Molly Bellman.
WPC. Joyce Carlett (First Wallasey WPC).
WPC. Marie Cushing (Came from Liverpool City Police).
WPC. Barbara Gale, became an Inspector with the Liverpool City Force.
WPC. G Garett.
WPC. Lillian EA (Betty) Daulman
WPC. Linda JT Elliott.
WPC. Joyce Esseen.
WPC. Joyce Garnet Evans.
WPC. June Evans.
WPC. Valerie Fuge.
WPC. Gillian Hopewell.
WPC.17 (5) MB Hutchinson.
WPC. Barbara Jones.
WPC. Brenda Parkes (Came from Liverpool City Police).
WPC. Thelma Rogers.
WPC. Violet Samson.
WPC. Norah Walbell.
WPC. Brenda Woodward.
WPC. Veronica Warrington.

Three unofficial WPCs who dressed in uniform for lecturing purposes etc.:-
Noelle Worrall, Gertrude McKay and Gertrude Herron.
Lill Dawson, Miss Hughes and Noelle Worrall looked after the switchboard.

Commandants of the Special Constabulary
Sir Thomas David Owen.
Mr Cyril H Newport, MBE – Deputy Captain G Nickson.
Mr Frank L Wilson.
Mr Fredrick VW Crook BEM. – Deputy Mr H Beggs.

A small selection of officers who were in Wallasey with the Cheshire or Merseyside Force, some who are still with the present-day Force:-
Chief Superintendent Thomas H Carter.

Chief Superintendent Ronald Garnett.
Chief Superintendent Clifford Halsall.
Chief Superintendent William Beasley.
Superintendent Robert Hughes.
Superintendent Stephen Cahill.
Superintendent Brian McIver.
Det. Supertintendent Desmond Green.
Chief Inspector Ronald Beech.
Chief Inspector John Cook.
Det.Insp. John Calligan.
Insp.   AW Lewis.
Insp.   Gordon Owen.
Insp.   T Ridley.
Sgt.   Micheal Carr.
Sgt.   B Faulker.
Sgt.   P Mather.
Sgt.   R Rawklinson.
Sgt.   AF ('Swasie') Turner.
Sgt.   T Wiliams.
Det.Sgt. George Davies.
Det.Sgt. Paula Parker.
DC.   Frank Anderson.
PC.   – Arfell.
PC.   Timothy Baldock.
PC.   J Behan.
PC.   – Berry.
PC.   Steven Blakemore.
PC.   E Brabin.
PC.   CD Brown.
PC.   – Byers.
PC.   D Byron.
PC.   WNO Carr.
PC.   Frank Chapman.
PC.   Robert Chapman.
PC.   Paul Chesters.
PC.   John Clayton.
PC.   Malcolm Cook.
PC.   F Corker.
PC.   Michael Craven
PC.   Reginald Joseph Dobson.
PC.   P Dutton.
PC.   Alan Edwards.
PC.   James Edwards.
PC.   R Evans.
PC.   Peter Flanagan.
PC.   R Faulkner.
PC.   George F Ferrier.
PC.   John Fletcher.
PC.   E Fletcher.
DC.   Simon Fritzpatrick.
PC.   Alan Hamilton.
PC.   – Hankey.
PC.   Russel P Hansard.
DC.   Russell Harper.
PC.   J Harrison.
PC.   – Hibbert.
PC.   Alan Higgs.
DC.   Geoff Higgs.
PC.   Bernard Higgins.
PC.   T Hodgson.
DC.   Vincent Howcroft.
PC.100 T Roy Humphreys.
PC.   – Humphries.
PC.   S Hurton.
PC.   S Jackson.

PC.   Neville Johnson.
PC.   K Johnstone.
PC.   P Johnstone.
PC.   – Jones.
PC.   Sean Kehoe.
PC.   C Kemp.
PC.   C Kent.
PC.   H Keown.
PC.   H Laughley.
PC.   – Look.
PC.   Ron Mahon.
PC.   Eric Marshall.
PC.   A Morris, later Detective Sergeant.
PC.   John Morris.
PC.   M Mears.
PC.   G Mitton.
PC.   M Morrell.
PC.   Kevin McGuinty.
PC.   Phillip McCarten.
PC.   Raymond Newnes.
PC.   David Owens.
PC.   Mark Phillips.
PC.   M Porter.
PC.   Horace Pointon.
PC.   N Price.
PC.   R Pritchard
PC.   Steven Quale.
PC.   Keith Raybould.
PC.   – Richards.
PC.   Alan Richotts, became Sergeant.
DC.   T Rimmer.
PC.   – Roughley.
PC.   C Royden.
PC. 31 Charles Rycroft.
PC.   K Shield.
PC.   A Smith.
PC.   Phillip Smith, became Sergeant.
PC.   Charles Taylor.
PC.   George Thomas.
PC.   Leonard Thompson.
PC.   Ian Thornton.
PC.   Micheal Wearing.
PC.   Peter Wherley, became Sergeant at Birkenhead.
PC.   P Whelan.

WPC. Elizabeth Allan.
WPC. Pamela Ashcroft.
WPC. T Bellinger
WPC. Marjory Coffee.
WPC. Tara Davey.
WPC. – Fenna.
WCP. Lesley Farlam.
WPC. Michelle Hogg.
WPC. – Guy.
WPC. Sybil Hardacre.
WPC. – Kerr.
WPC. Sarah Micklewright.
WPC. Lesley Rennie.
WPC   Tracy Waring.
WPC. Amanda Wiesenekker.

ANNUAL POLICE RIVER SWIM
List of Winners

Year	Winner	Year	Winner
1921	Det.Con Frank Peck.	1966	Con. W Whitfield.
1922	Con. James Warner.	1967	Con. GF Ferrier.
1923	Det. Con.Frank Peck.	1968	Con. J Whitfield.
1924	Det. Con. Frank Peck.	1969	Con. J Whitfield.
1925	Con. Robert H Jackson.	1970	Con. Alan Steen.
1926	Con. David N Starkey.	1971	Con. Alan Steen.
1927	Con. David N Starkey.	1972	Con. Alan Williams.
1928	Con. David N Starkey.	1973	Con. Alan Williams.
1929	Sgt. Charles T Sandland.	1974	Con. Alan Williams.
1930	Sgt. Charles T Sandland.	1975	Con. Alan Williams.
1931	Sgt. Charles T Sandland.	1976	Con. Alan Williams.
1932	Insp. Charles T Sandland.	1977	Con.Alan Williams
1933	Con. Ernest Warrington.	1978	Con. Alan Williams.
1934	Con. Ernest Warrington.	1979	Con. Alan Williams.
1935	Con. Ernest Warrington.	1980	Con. Alan Williams.
1936	Con. Ernest Warrington.	1982	Con. Sean J Kehoe.
1937	Con. Ernest Warrington.	1983	Con. Sean J Kehoe.
1938	Con. Ernest Warrington.	1984	Con. Sean J Kehoe.
1939	Con. Ernest Warrington (if held).		
		1985	Con. Sean J Kehoe.
1952	Cancelled.	1986	Con. Sean J Kehoe.
1953	Sgt. Ernest Warrington.	1987	Con. Sean J Kehoe.
1954	Sgt. Ernest Warrington.	1988	Con. Sean J Kehoe.
1955	Sgt. Ernest Warrington.	1989	Con. Sean J Kehoe.
1966	Insp. Ernest Warrington.	1990	Con. Sean J Kehoe.
1957	Insp. Ernest Warrington.	1991	Con. Sean J Kehoe.
1958	Insp. Ernest Warrington.	1992	Con. Sean J Kehoe.
1959	Insp. Ernest Warrington.	1993	Con. Sean J Kehoe.
1960	Insp. Ernest Warrington.	1994	Con. Sean J Kehoe.
1961	Insp. Ernest Warrington.	1995	Con. Sean J Kehoe.
1962	Con. Phillip S Smith.	1996	ConTimothy Baldock.
1963	Con. PA Pinnington.	1997	Con. Steve Blakemore.
1964	Con. PA Pinnington.	1998	Con. Steve Blakemore.
1965	Con. PA Pinnington.	1999	Not competed for.
		2000/1	Not competed for.

******

APPENDIX II

Chief Fire Officers Wallasey Fire Brigade

Year	
1889	Captain WT Leather
1895	Superintendent John Howarth
1902	Superintendent GW Byne
1918	Chief Fire Officer William H Nicholson
1948	Chief Fire Officer Joseph Holt, QFSM
1963	Chief Fire Officer Ernest E Buschenfeld, MBE

Some of the Firemen that served at Wallasey in addition to the Police Firemen listed earlier:-

Early days:-

Sgt. Abraham Halewood.   Fireman John Walker.
Sgt.Peter Leather.   =   John Fellowes.
Sgt. William Clark   =   Harold Gibbons.
Sgt. Joseph Dodd   =   Robert Francis Herron
Fireman George Addison.   (as in Police List).
  =   John Bleakley.   =   Henry Holder.
  =   Arthur Thomas Boyle.   =   Herbert Johnson.
  =   John Bushell (Driver).   =   George Joughin.
  =   D Campbell.   =   James Lea.
  =   Robert Carson.   =   William Henry Liversage.
  =   W Davies   =   James Shone (Killed whilst on duty).

  =   John Dutton.   =   Thomas Somerville.
                 =   Herbert Winstanley (I).

From Circa 1913 to Circa 1939:-
Senior Company Officer Stafford Donning.
Company Officer George Mercer.
Sgt.   – Vyne.
Sgt.   Joseph Holdsworth.
Engineer – Barnby
  =   Ernest Lindsay Paton.
  =   Ernest Platt.
Fireman Leonard A Barnes.
  =   John Beech.
  =   Patrick Casey.
  =   Harold Cash, became Deputy Chief Fire Officer.
  =   Frank James Cooper. Ex-Acton Brigade. War-time at Wallasey.
  =   Isaac Cowan.
  =   Clinch.
  =   – Driscoll.
  =   Frank Fradley. From Police. (Became Deputy Chief Fire Officer).
  =   Thomas Garner, NFS.
  =   John Glover.
  =   Robert Johnson.
  =   Edward Jones.
  =   Walter H Meacock (appointed Sub-Officer).
  =   Henry McMinn.
  =   Samuel Pemberton (became Sub-Officer).
  =   Samuel GA Pink.
  =   William Ormbsby Pooley.
  =   John Price.
  =   Herbert Winstanley (II) (became Sergeant).
  =   John Winstanley (Became Station Officer).
  =   Leslie Stanley Winstanley.
Mr Stafford Donning took over from Colin Sanders as Commandant of the Auxiliaries and Mr George Mercer as Deputy.
Also see Police/Firemen.

Circa 1940 to Circa 1945:-
Fireman Micheal Joseph Cleary.
  =   Edward Colpin.
  =   Douglas Cooper.
  =   George Davies.
  =   William Davies.
  =   Percy Dearing.
  =   Henry David Driscoll.
  =   Frank Feryhough (became an Ambulance Driver).
  =   RW Giles.
  =   Max Haliwell.
  =   Robert Charles Hawley.
  =   George Harrison (Died as a result of bombing).
  =   Thomas Henry Howard.
  =   Albert Charles James.
  =   Harry Johnson.
  =   Harold Jones.
  =   Cecil Kesteron.
  =   Harry Mell.
  =   Thomas Nichols.
  =   Oliver Brown Phillips.
  =   Sydney Pope.
  =   Ernest Richings (Killed in air-raids).
  =   Bill Rivers.
  =   Thomas Henry Roberts (Died as result of the bombing).
  =   William Roberts.

= George Roche.
= William Rogerson from Lancashire (Killed in air-raids).
= John Smyth.
= John Trott.
= Harry Walker.
= Herbert Winstanley (III).

N.B.
It is to be understood there was a large number of Full and Part-Time NFS men during the Second World. The above is just a small number of them. I apologise for not including others that did gallant work during the air-raids.

Cira 1945 to take-over:-
Harold Lacy, Fire Prevention Officer, became ADO. Returned to Wallasey.
JW Rothwell, came to Wallasey as Station Officer in 1964.
Fire Prevention Officer Harold Chapman.
Fireman – Adey.
= William Agnew (became Station Officer).
= R Alexandra.
= James Askey.
= RJ Aspey.
= William Asquith.
= Brian Badley.
= D Baguly.
= Alfred Barker.
= George Bateman, Mechanic (became Sub-Officer).
= Gordon R Beck (became ADO).
= Harry Beck.
= Ronald Beck (all brothers).
= Robert Begg (became Column Officer).
= Maurice Bennard.
= Charles Best (joined 1946. Ex-Navy).
= D Broster.
= Anthony Brown AFS.
= Ronald Burrows.
= Michael N Carr.
= K Charnley.
= John Clement.
= – Clinch.
= AR Cook (became Sub-Officer).
= Michael Connor.
= Edward Currie (Emmigarted to New Zealand).
= WE Corry.
= DH Dawson.
= Leslie ('Dabs') Derbyshire .
= Alec P ('Dixie') Dean, went to Westmorland. Returned to Wallasey as ADO, later Deputy Chief Officer. Merseyside as DO later SDO.
= Dave Douglas.
= John Dunlop.
= Gethin Lewellyn Edwards (became Station Officer).
= Colin Edwards.
= John Ellison.
= James W Evans.
= Robert Evans (became Chief Officer with Hampshire Fire Brigade).
= VPR Fitzsimmons (became Station Officer).
= TW Fleming.
= Reginald Font.
= William Forber.
= Charles Foster.
= Kevin Foxley (became Station Officer).
= Dave Franklin (became ADO in Merseyside Fire Brigade).

= Alfred Gale.
= Keith Garner.
= Thomas Gorman.
= Charles W Graham.
= R Grogan (became DO).
= David Hardland.
= LG Hardman (became Sub-Officer).
= Robert Harland.
= Andrew Harper.
= Kenneth Harrison (became Station Officer. Later at Hoylake)
= Micheal Harris.
= Norman Harwood.
= R Hazelhurst.
= ('Jock') Higgins.
= William Higham.
= KA Hollis (became Station Officer).
= Arthur Horace.
= Terrance Howells.
= Bill Hughes.
= D Hunt.
= Ronald James.
= Micheal Johnson.
= David Glynn Jones, (bacame ADO).
= David Leonard Jones (became DO).
= Edward Newton Jones (became Station Officer).
= Michael Jones.
= James E Joy (became Sub Officer).
= Donald Kelly, (became ADO - Senior Fire Prevention Officer)
= OM Keough (became Sub-Officer).
= Joseph Killoran (became AFO)
= B Kingey.
= Terrance W Langton (became Sub Officer).
= Walter Leach.
= James Lee, Senior Watch Room Attendant.
= William Ledder.
= David John Liston (became Sub-Officer).
= Kenneth London (became Sub Officer).
= Vincent Lynn (became a JP).
= John Edward McEneany (went into the Ambulance Service).
= M McKillop (became Station officer).
= WJ Manning.
= David Martindale (went to Northampton).
= Bernard A Masters, BEM. Came from Worcester.
= Samuel Mealer, became Commander of Western Divion, Merseyside.
= Robert Mercer.
= Raymond George Milns (became Station Officer)..
= Sidney A Molyneux.
= Clifford Moore.
= Malcolm Munro.
= Barry Murdoch.
= JA Murray.
= Norman Newton, Section Leader.
= AA Palmer (became Station Officer).
= Alfred Parker.
= Brian Parry (became Station officer).
= Allan Peers.
= Alfred Pennington.
= R Peters.
= Edward Phillips, joined as Police/Fireman.
= RE Phillips.
= Samuel Pink Jr., (became an Officer in the South).
= RW Preston (became Sub-Officer).

=   Colin Price.
=   John Price.
=   David Pritchard (became Sub-Officer).
=   Leslie E Pugh.
=   D Pulford.
=   R Pulson.
=   Lewis Bevin ('Taffy') Redmore (became Sub-Officer).
=   Derek R Redmore Jnr. (son of 'Taffy' above - became Sub-Officer).
=   Cyril Redmore Jnr. (son of 'Taffy' above).
=   Timothy Riley, became Station Officer.
=   Joseph Cyril Roberts.
=   GF Rogan (from Police).
=   Hugh Ross.
=   Thomas Rutter.
=   Jack Sheen.
=   Noel Stead, became ACO, Merseyside.
=   Bert Smith.
=   GH Smith.
=   John A Smith.
=   Alec Steen, became an Officer.
=   James T Taylor.
=   Kenneth Thompson.
=   Barry H Tingey.
=   Geffrey Toland.
=   Francis Patrick Uriel, became ADO, later SDO in the Eastern Division.
=   W Walls.
=   Richard J Wainwright.
=   Stanley Watkins.
=   Thomas West.
=   Dave Williams.
=   Robert Williams.
=   Christopher Wilkinson.
=   William ('Ginger') Whitfield.
=   Kenneth E Woods.
=   John Wright, became Station Officer.
Mechanic David Todd (workshop).
Maintainance Richard Campbell.
Maintainance Joseph Williams.

Firewomen Control Staff:-
Bernadette Davies (Leading Firewoman).
Pamela Davies.
P Francis Dutton.
Joan Dyer (Beck).
Frances Howard (AFS, served during the Second World War).
Glynis B Lomax (became ADO).
Dianne Longworth (Gornall).
Kathleen A McGeah.
Marion Nolan (Rose) (became Asst. Control Officer).
Margaret Poole (West).
Hilary Porter.
Pamela Staples.
B Williams.
Joan Williams.
JM Yates.

Ambulance Personel:-

No.1 John Steen.	10 Cliffordd Done	19 Leslie Brereton.
2 Bert Matthews.	11 Albert Garner.	20 Gordon Duxbury.
3 Lian Jones.	12 Frank Fernyhough	21 Trevor Morgan.
4 Thomas Salter.	13 Harold Mathews.	22 Frank Smith.
5 Frank Whitby.	14 Jame Tierney.	23 Alfred Cross.
6 Wilfred Borne.	15 William Jones.	24 Harold Charles Ellett.
7 Samuel Pink.	16 William Roy Parry.	Phillip Hardy.
8 Samuel Court.	17 John Evans.	Vincent Lee.
9 Sidney Gracy.	18 Frank Mather.	Brian Boyd.
		W Halliday.

FLEET LIST
Appliances until 1973:

c.1875	Hand-Drawn Hose Carts.	
1898	Horse-Drawn Manual Pump *	
1898	Horse-Drawn Escape	
1899	Merryweather Horse-Drawn Steam Pump	
1900	Merryweather Horse-Drawn Chemical Engine Pump/ Escape.	
1914	Dennis-Tamini Motor Pump-Escape	Reg.No. HF 89 (?)
1915	Leyland-Mather & Platt Motor Pump	Reg.No. HF 93
1930	BSA Motor Cycle with side-car	Reg.No. HF 278**
1935	Leyland FK4 'Cub' Pump	Reg.No. HF 4730
c.1939	Leyland Pump	Reg No. –
c.1942	Austin Utility Vehicle with Heavy Leyland Pump	Reg.No. –
1942	Bedford Escape with front pump	Reg.No. GXN 245
1948	Austin K4-Merryweather 60ft. Turn-Table P Ex-NFS	Reg.No. –
1948	Austin-Leyland-Tangye Major Pump ex NFS	Reg.No.–
1948	Austin K2 Auxiliary Towing Vehicle (van)Ex-NFS	Reg.No. GLT 441
c.1953	Bedford Self-Propelled Pumps (Green Goddess)	
–	Ditto –	
1953	Dennis F12 Major Pump-Escape	Reg.No. BHF 556
1954	Dennis F8 Pump	Reg.No. CHF 606
1958	Dennis F24 Pump-Escape (Yellow livery)	Reg.No. FHF 60
1960	AEC-Merryweather 100ft. Turn-Table Platform	Reg.No. HHF 84
1962	Ford Van	Reg.No. LHF 305
1963	Vauxhall Staff Car	Reg.No. MHF 384
1965	Commer General Purpose Van	Reg.No.AHF 629C
1965	Ford Van	Reg.No BHF 438C
1966	Vauxhall Staff Car	Reg.No CHF 601D
1968	Commer Emergency Tender	Reg.No. –
1969	Morris Van	Reg.No GHF 289G
1969	Morris-Mini General Purpose Van	Reg.No GHF 268G
1969	Dennis F44 Pump-Escape (Yellow livery)	Reg.No HHF 107H
1971	Dennis F43 Pump (Yellow livery)	Reg.No. JHF 707J
1972	Dennis Emergency Tender with front winch	Reg.No. LHF 75K
c.1972	5 cwt.Towed Trailer.	
1972	Ford Transit Van	Reg.No MHF 2856
1972	Ford Transit General Purpose Lorry.	Reg.No MHF 285L
1972	Ford Staff Car	Reg.No LHF 675K
1972	Morris Mini Van	RegNoGHF 1268G
1972	Morris-Mini General Purpose Van	Reg.No LHF 594K

Part of Merseyside Fire Brigade 27/3/1974.
Appliances included:-

Dennis	F44 Pump Escape	Reg.No. F 933 YCM.
Dennis	F44 Pump Escape	Reg.No. H 150 GBG.
Dennis	'R' Series Pump	Reg.No. NHF 288S.

A Ford V8 Fordson Escape Carrier with Front-Mounted Pump was also used in the 1950s.

* The Wallasey Fire Brigade was involved in the dispute at the Egremont Brickworks in 1877. It is not clear whether a Hand-Drawn Fire Cart was used or a Hose-drawn Fire Engine.
** Reg. No. HF278 was transferred from another vehicle.